THE G[...]
ACCORDING TO
ST. PAUL

MEDITATIONS ON HIS LIFE AND LETTERS

THE GOSPEL ACCORDING TO ST. PAUL

MEDITATIONS ON HIS LIFE AND LETTERS

CARDINAL

CARLO MARIA MARTINI, SJ

Translated by Marsha Daigle-Williamson, PhD

Originally published in 2007 by Ancora Editrice, Milan, Italy, as
Il Vangelo di Paolo, copyright © 2007 Ancora S.r.l.
English translation copyright © 2008 The Word Among Us Press.
All rights reserved.

Published in the United States and Canada by The Word Among Us Press
9639 Doctor Perry Road
Ijamsville, Maryland 21754
www.wordamongus.org
12 11 10 09   3 4 5 6
ISBN: 978-1-59325-145-1

Cover design by John Hamilton Design

El Greco (Domenikos Theotokopulos) Saint Paul. c. 1608-14.
Location: Museo del Prado, Madrid, Spain
Photo Credit: Erich Lessing/Art Resource, NY

Library of Congress Cataloging-in-Publication Data
Martini, Carlo Maria, 1927-
[Vangelo di Paolo. English]
The Gospel according to St. Paul : meditations on his life and letters /
Carlo Maria Martini.
     p. cm.
ISBN 978-1-59325-145-1 (alk. paper)
1. Paul, the Apostle, Saint--Meditations. 2. Bible. N.T. Epistles of Paul--
Meditations. I. Title. II. Title: Gospel according to Saint Paul.
BS2506.3.M3613 2008
225.9'2--dc22
[B]
                                          2008007387

CONTENTS

FOREWORD

The biblical reflections on the life and writings of St. Paul contained in this book are characteristic of the sensitive combination of devoted scholarship and pastoral spirit possessed by Cardinal Carlo Maria Martini, SJ. In these pages, Martini provides insight, commentary, and meditations on key moments in Paul's life and key passages in his writings that are designed to stimulate the mind and penetrate the heart. Martini's reflections are especially timely, given the fact that Pope Benedict XVI has declared a year dedicated to St. Paul, beginning on June 29, 2008.

Cardinal Carlo Martini has had an enormous influence on the Church's mission to increase biblical literacy and devotion among Catholics. I came to be influenced by Martini's work through his three intertwined vocations as biblical scholar, Jesuit priest, and pastoral leader. After receiving his doctorate in sacred Scripture, he lived the academic life of a professor of Scripture. He soon became rector of the Pontifical Biblical Institute in Rome. It is there that I was privileged to be his student during my graduate school days in biblical studies.

During his time at the Pontifical Biblical Institute, he coordinated the work of some of the Church's finest scholars and produced teachers of the Bible who are working today throughout the world. Though he was always accessible to students and faculty, he never failed to take his deserved sabbatical for more intensive research and writing. As a first-rate scholar with an inspiring devotion to the sacred text, he always sought to connect academic study with the life of Christian discipleship.

As a Jesuit priest, Carlo Martini found the path of his discipleship by following in the way of St. Ignatius of Loyola. All Jesuits learn, through the *Spiritual Exercises* of St. Ignatius, to personalize the Scriptures so that they have an impact upon their individual lives. The method of meditation encouraged by Ignatius invites Christians to use their imagination to visualize the biblical scene, to imagine what the five senses would have experienced in the situation, and to imaginatively and emotionally respond to the encounter expressed by the biblical text.

A Jesuit is a contemplative in action, and Carlo Martini always teaches about the Bible out of this Ignatian spirituality. Meditating on a biblical text moves the reader toward discernment, decision, and action. Jesuit spirituality is a practical holiness that helps people live their ordinary lives with a divine perspective, always seeking to discern God's movements in the concrete reality of life. This type of biblical meditation helps to gradually transform people from passivity to a passionate love for God and a commitment to God's reign. This is the kind of active contemplation that Carlo Martini knows to be the goal of biblical reflection.

After his academic life in the universities of Rome, Carlo Martini was chosen by Pope John Paul II as the archbishop of Milan. Three years later he was named a cardinal of the Church. After some young people in his diocese asked him to teach them how to pray with the Bible, he formed the School of the Word in his cathedral. These monthly gatherings became so popular that the cathedral soon overflowed with young people; the meetings were then broadcast by radio to gatherings in churches throughout the diocese.

At these gatherings Cardinal Martini used a group form of the ancient practice of *lectio divina* (sacred reading). The sessions usually began with the chanting of a psalm to create the atmosphere of prayerful listening. The group was then encouraged to listen attentively to the reading of a passage from the Bible. The readings were selected from the topics chosen by the cardinal for his series. For example, a few sessions on the prayers of the Bible would be followed by a series on God's call in Scripture, then themes from Paul's writings, and so on. The reading of the text was then followed by Martini's explanation and his guided reflections on the meaning and message of the passage. Finally, the group spent time in silent contemplation—fifteen minutes of absolute quiet for individual reflection and prayer.

Cardinal Martini insisted that the secret of the School of the Word's success was that he did not offer the young people a homily or catechism lesson. Rather, he facilitated their encounter with Scripture. The sessions taught the students to meditate personally on the text, and it gave them a taste for the workings of the Holy Spirit in the word of God. When they learned to discover their own insights and to discern the relationship of the text to their own lives and then felt stimulated to pray, they experienced an interior joy. Then, with their appetite for sacred reading of Scripture whetted, they continued to discover the richness of Scripture through their own meditation and prayer.

More than two decades after studying under Carlo Martini, I became reacquainted with his work in practicing and promoting the ancient art of *lectio divina*. As I began to teach and write about this time-honored way of praying the Scriptures, I realized that Cardinal Martini was one of the key players in reviving it for the Church today. I was so inspired by his apostolic zeal for Scripture that I dedicated my book *Conversing with God in Scripture: A Contemporary Approach to Lectio Divina* (The Word Among Us Press, 2008) to Cardinal Martini.

This archbishop of Milan knew the ancient art of *lectio divina*, nurtured in the monasteries throughout Christian history, and he revitalized its practice in new ways for contemporary people. He knew that the traditional phases of reading, meditation, prayer, and contemplation led to interior transformation, but he also knew that the word of God can transform the world. He understood that prayerful reflection on Scripture in the light of Christ, just as in the life of Paul, leads to discernment, deliberation, and action.

Carlo Martini—biblical scholar, Jesuit priest, and pastoral leader—has deeply influenced my own life, and I know he can inspire yours as you read his work. After more than eighty years of life, this now-retired cardinal continues to be transformed by praying the Scriptures and continues to lead many into a fruitful conversation with God through the sacred text.

Stephen J. Binz

Preface to the Italian Edition

Over the years, many people, including priests, religious, lay people, and youth, in very diverse contexts, have been nourished by the retreats and spiritual exercises guided by Cardinal Martini. Scripture passages that are heard in prayerful silence and interpreted in the light of his experience as a pastor point the way to an authentic spiritual life for whoever seeks to deepen his or her vocation. This work is still being carried on because Martini, now living in Jerusalem, has not stopped teaching the Word and participating in spiritual events.

It is not surprising that an alert editor understood the usefulness of collecting some of the cardinal's writings on the recurring topics that drew his attention at various times and places during his pastoral ministry in Milan. The figure of the apostle Paul is certainly one of these recurring topics, as this collection demonstrates, and this book is dedicated to Cardinal Martini on his eightieth birthday.

I was present for almost all the preaching that gave rise to these chapters in which it seems that Paul himself is being heard "in the midst of his ministry," as one of the chapters says. Martini's preaching reveals the growth of Paul's passion for the gospel, his dedication to the communities that formed around his apostolic preaching, and his obvious love for Jesus. Service to the gospel, which is carried out today through multiple vocations, is described with the certainty that inspires it, the trials that accompany it, and the hope in which it is rooted. The cardinal listens to Paul, but at the same time, he gives a voice and a face to those who are engaged in the apostolic endeavors of the Church today. Reading these pages, we can often recognize ourselves and find ourselves helped.

Because of this, the apostle to the Gentiles becomes, in the cardinal's skillful interpretation, a "companion for the journey" for so many today who serve the gospel of Jesus with joy.

Don Franco Brovelli
Author and Vicar for Continuing Education of the Clergy
Diocese of Milan, Italy

PART I
SERVANT OF CHRIST JESUS

CHAPTER 1

Paul's Conversion

I would like to look more closely at the Damascus event, just as Paul did later in some of his letters. I confess a hesitation to delve into the mystery of God in another person, even though Paul is a representative figure for all of Christianity.

I also freely confess an inability to fully capture the meaning of the texts. May the Lord grant me mercy and help me understand some part of the indescribable light that enveloped Paul and transformed the life of this apostle.

To understand the richness of the divine action in Paul, to understand what he said about his experience that millions of people refer to, we need to reflect on three descriptions of his conversion that are found in the Acts of the Apostles: chapter 9 (in a third person account) and chapters 22 and 26 (in autobiographical form).

The description in chapter 26 has the greatest number of autobiographical details, and it is also the most popular and complete account. This is the last speech Paul made: his defense before Agrippa in Caesarea. It can serve as the departure point to clarify what questions we should ask Paul and to hear the answers he gives in passages from the Acts of the Apostles and some of his letters.

The remains of Agrippa's imperial palace have recently been discovered. It is precisely in that spot, near the sea, where the waves break against the ruins of Roman buildings today, that Paul said this about himself:

I myself was convinced that I ought to do many things [he had a strong sense of duty] in opposing the name of Jesus of Nazareth. And I did so in Jerusalem; I not only shut up many of the saints in prison, by authority from the chief priests, but when they were put to death I cast my vote against them. [The case he refers to evidently concerns Stephen and the approval he gave to Stephen's death, even if he himself did not throw any stones.] And I punished them often in all the synagogues and tried to make them blaspheme; and in raging fury against them, I persecuted them even to foreign cities. (Acts 26:9-11)

At this point, some historical problems need to be addressed. It does not seem that the Sanhedrin at that time had any power outside the synagogues of Palestine, and the synagogues themselves had limited powers—certainly not the power to put people to death. The very killing of Stephen is probably an action they decided upon on their own as a result of popular uprising, and it was outside of the law. Synagogues could interrogate, scourge, and impose different kinds of penalties; this is the milieu in which Paul was initially operating. Historians, therefore, are dubious about the phrase "foreign cities." Perhaps Paul had procured for himself some letters of recommendation and, with a zeal that surpassed that of almost anybody else, went to those cities to convince them to persecute Christians. He was a man gifted with great creativity when he was pursuing what seemed right to him.

Thus I journeyed to Damascus with the authority and commission of the chief priests. At midday, O king, I saw on the way a light from heaven, brighter than the sun, shining round me and those who journeyed with me. (Acts 26:12-13)

The phrase we need to pay attention to is "a light from heaven." Paul meditated a great deal on that light and returned to it in writing to the Corinthians: "For it is . . . God who said, 'Let light shine out of darkness,' who has shone in our hearts" (2 Corinthians 4:6).

The God who created all light manifested himself with an even greater light: Paul links all of God's great creative actions in the Old Testament with what has happened in him—a profound burst of light whose source is the glory of Christ himself, in the light of which all else pales.

> And when we had all fallen to the ground, I heard a voice saying to me in the Hebrew language, "Saul, Saul, why do you persecute me? It hurts you to kick against the goads." And I said, "Who are you, Lord?" And the Lord said, "I am Jesus whom you are persecuting. But rise and stand upon your feet; for I have appeared to you for this purpose, to appoint you to serve and bear witness to the things in which you have seen me and to those in which I will appear to you, delivering you from the people and from the Gentiles—to whom I send you to open their eyes, that they may turn from darkness to light and from the power of Satan to God, that they may receive forgiveness of sins and a place among those who are sanctified by faith in me." (Acts 26:14-18)

Adding this text to the others, we can ask Paul a few questions:

■ What place did the Lord make you leave in order to bring you to Damascus, and what was your situation when the Word of God came to you?

■ In what direction did this foundational event of your life take you?

■ How did this transition occur, i.e., your passing over from death to life, from darkness to light, from not knowing God to knowing God?

What Was Paul's Situation When the Word Came to Him?

The answer is found in an autobiographical text in the Letter to the Philippians. Paul affirms here that the Word of God took hold of him at a time when he possessed fundamental goods that were precious to him and had been acquired, in part, at a steep price: "I myself have reason for confidence in the flesh also" (Philippians 3:4a). He is referring to the things that belong to him because of his own nature, his history, and his activities: "If any other man thinks he has reason for confidence in the flesh, I have more" (3:4b). These are the elements Paul lists, which belong to his distinguished history:

—*Circumcised on the eighth day (3:5)*: I was not like the pagans, disdainfully called the "uncircumcised" in the sense of being cursed, abandoned—those for whom God seems not to have any concern;

—*Of the people of Israel (3:5)*: I came from the elect people, the light of the nations;

—*Of the tribe of Benjamin (3:5)*: I knew my heritage, my ancestors, the links that connected me to the son of Jacob;

—*A Hebrew born of Hebrews (3:5)*: I had a rich heritage, that is, father, mother, grandparents, all from this illustrious family line;

—*As to the law a Pharisee (3:5)*: I was a strictly observant Hebrew who knew the law completely and carried it out with the most absolute moral rigor as I lived out the profound spiritual tensions of Judaism. "Pharisee" was a glorious name that emphasized commitment to a life lived under the law with a great inner sense of duty;

—*As to zeal a persecutor of the church, as to righteousness under the law, blameless (3:6)*: This latter phrase is the same praise that is given to Joseph, the righteous man. The parents of John the Baptist, Zechariah and Elizabeth, are also described this way: they were both righteous (Luke 1:6). Paul applies to himself the highest praise that can be given from the biblical point of view;

—Blameless: I could have asked, "Who among you can convict me of sin?"

—There was nothing in me that could be faulted from the perspective of the law: We know how minute the commandments and the ceremonial statutes were and how complicated the rituals were. Even today a Jewish meal is very complicated, with many rules about foods, the combinations of foods to avoid, and foods whose origins need to be certified. This kind of focus calls for intense spiritual effort.

Paul finds himself, then, possessing traditions, personal commitment, zeal, and righteousness. These great goods are immensely precious to him, and he lists them with deep emotion. One needs to be acquainted with the Jews to understand the intensity with which, even today, they declare themselves Jews and confess their family roots and their tradition. It is something that is second nature to them, so much so that it cannot be renounced.

The perfect example is Simone Weil. She intuited in the most profound manner the mysteries of baptism, Eucharist, and prayer.

She wrote pages that are perhaps among the most beautiful on Christian life, on work, on contemplation, but she was never baptized, because it seemed impossible to her to renounce her Jewish identity. Despite profoundly intuiting the beauty of Christian truth and longing to nourish herself with the Eucharist—which she genuinely recognized as the culmination of history and of creation—in the end, she was blocked by the richness of what she felt she possessed and by the need for solidarity with her tormented people.

Paul uses an expression that refers to Jesus in the Letter to the Philippians, but certainly in this context, it could have an autobiographical flavor: "Christ Jesus, . . . though he was in the form of God, did not count equality with God a thing to be grasped" (Philippians 2:5-6). The Greek text seems to mean, "Jesus did not consider it as a prize," that is, as an avid possession to greedily keep for himself. Paul was relating to his heritage in the opposite way; it was a jealously guarded treasure that could not be surrendered to anyone. Having this possession led to a great concern to defend it, a great zeal to promote it, and great violence against those who might threaten it.

This explains Paul's intolerance of Christians and his need to exterminate them because he understood, rightly so, that they were challenging precisely the root of that treasure.

We can now understand his self-accusations that are later reported in the First Letter to Timothy: "I formerly blasphemed and persecuted and insulted him [Christ]" (1:13). He was not a blasphemer in the sense that he was turning away from God, but in the sense that, without knowing it—and his whole conversion, the drama that he lived, lies in this—he was indeed turning away from Christ, the Son of God, in defending his precious treasure. In light of this, we can understand why he described his life as lived in sin because, in reality—and he will be aware of it more and more—his attitude toward God was profoundly wrong. He did not consider God to be God, the author and originator of every good. The center of everything for him was what belonged to him—his own truth, the treasures that had been entrusted to him. This was an approach that was externally blameless, but internally it was based on extreme possessiveness, to such a degree that it struck at the root of his relationship with God, the Father and Creator.

This is the distortion that he was living without knowing it; out of it would arise his new understanding of the gospel, of grace, of mercy, of the divine initiative, and of God's action. He was not living the gospel of grace but rather the law of self-justification, which made him forget that he was only a human being, blessed by God, not because he was anything in himself, but because God loved him.

Paul's story is the difficult story of a person who is profoundly religious, but whose religious approach threatens to lead him to a radical distortion of the image of God.

This is the place from which Paul and his violent ideology come. Ideological violence, the fruit of fanaticism and of the inability to understand others unless they are submitted to the same ideals, has not disappeared in our times. People are still seeking to save themselves, are still seeking a righteousness and a self-justification that leads to every kind of aberration because of a "treasure" that leads them to believe they are the owners, and not the servants, of the truth.

Paul's situation is instructive with regard to some of the most profound perversions; Jesus confronts that in the gospel when he says, "[Sinners] go into the kingdom of God before you" (see Matthew 21:31). This means that those who commit sin when, for instance, they get drunk or let themselves be overcome by sensuality, do commit sin, certainly, but they are always conscious of doing wrong. They need understanding, help, and mercy to overcome their failings and to confess that they are weak. Paul, instead, would never confess to failings or weakness. This is the very sin that Jesus connects to the Pharisees: the fundamental perversion of human beings seeking to save themselves and, believing themselves to have reached the pinnacle of perfection, of engaging in the worst kinds of violence.

In What Direction Was Paul Led?

Our second question for St. Paul is, "In what direction did the Lord take you?" Paul clarifies that direction for us in his letters to the Philippians and Galatians. First of all, the Lord led him to *a total detachment from what had formerly seemed most important to him:*

> But whatever gain I had, I counted as loss for the sake of Christ. Indeed I count everything as loss because of the surpassing worth of knowing Christ Jesus my Lord. For his sake I have suffered the loss of all things, and count them as refuse, in order that I may gain Christ. (Philippians 3:7-8)

This new direction leads him to realize that all his former goods count for nothing compared to Christ. It is not that they count for nothing in themselves, but in comparison with Christ they have no value.

It led him to a completely new vision of things. It led not to an immediate moral change but to an illumination: he speaks of revelation, because seeing from a new point of view—that of Christ—everything now appears different to him. He judges his life in such a new way that what best expresses his inner response to what Jesus tells him on the way to Damascus is this: "I have been wrong about everything. I believed some things to be valid that were not, which led me to behave in a violent and, in the end, unjust manner. Glorying in my own righteousness, I became an executioner of the innocent."

When Jesus asks Paul, "Why do you persecute me?" he suddenly understands that he has miserably confused the truth about things. Paul's terrible shock, not through logic but through a direct encounter with the truth, is understandable. He knows he has to redo and rethink everything from top to bottom. Matthew 13 describes similar situations: a merchant who found the pearl of great price realizes that everything else is worthless; the man who found a treasure hidden in a field realizes that nothing else has value now.

What happened to Paul was such a revelation of who Jesus is that it changed his mind and his attitude about who he himself was and what he was doing. It was a revelation that turned his inner orientation upside down.

The second way he describes this "new direction" is found especially in a chapter from the Letter to the Galatians: God "*was pleased to reveal his Son to me,* in order that I might preach him among the Gentiles" (1:16; italics added). This is the mission that was entrusted to Paul. It is shocking for Paul that these two things occur at the same time: the very moment Jesus makes him understand that he has been wrong about everything, he tells him, "I entrust everything to you; I send you."

The God of the gospel and of mercy, who in an instant makes me understand that I have been wrong about everything about him because I have put myself in his place, demonstrates his mercy toward me by forgiving me. Then he places his confidence in me by calling me into his service and entrusting his own Word to me.

That instant summarizes for Paul everything that he was mistaken about concerning God. Darkness becomes light; the violent man becomes merciful.

How Did Paul's Transition Occur?

But before speaking of conversion, we need to understand what was revealed and why Paul speaks of *revelation*.

Everything was given to him. His change was not due to his strength, meditation, spiritual exercises, long prayers, or fasting. Everything was given to him so that he could be for all peoples a *sign* of the merciful God, whose initiative always precedes our seeking.

It would be good to look again at Galatians 1:15-16, where Paul uses Old Testament language to describe what happened to him: "He who had set me apart before I was born, and had called me through his grace, was pleased to reveal his Son to me." The protagonist of the conversion is not Paul, it is God. All the action is on God's part; he is the author of conversion.

Just as in creation, when "God said . . . " and it came to be (see Genesis 1), so too it is God's initiative in conversion, far beyond any merit or desire or thought of our own.

God calls us and is pleased to manifest his Son to us. This is the first aspect of "how" the transition occurred: through grace, as a gift, because it pleased God.

Everything was given to him through knowing Jesus. We have already seen that Paul describes his conversion in terms of an encounter (1 Corinthians 15:8). Christ is the revelation of God's merciful initiative toward me. Christ is the encounter between Paul and God.

Questions to Ask Ourselves

■ What about my experience is similar, different, or analogous to Paul's experience?

■ How can I expect and receive the action or grace of God that makes me who I am?

■ How and in what way is Jesus (who for Paul is the revelation of divine mercy) the fundamental reference point for me to understand who I am, what I am, where I came from, and to what I am called?

■ What are the "treasures" that block me from freely responding to the divine initiative toward me?

We need to ask these questions in a spirit of love. If we ask them in a guarded or self-justifying spirit, we will answer them in haste, and we will not succeed in seeing our lives in depth under the gaze of God. But if we ask ourselves in a spirit of love and mercy, we will discover what in us is the work of God as well as what in us is like Paul's resistance to God's work.

Let us conclude with 1 Timothy 1:15: "The saying is sure and worthy of full acceptance, that Christ Jesus came into the world to save sinners. And I am the foremost of sinners."

The fundamental sin of human beings—the root of all sin—is the failure to acknowledge God as God, not recognizing his gift as the fruit of his love. It is the satanic attitude of opposition to God. Paul was refusing God's goodness to him under the banner of possessing good things.

All of us have that inability to acknowledge God as God.

And I am the foremost of sinners; but I received mercy for this reason, that in me, as the foremost, Jesus Christ might display his perfect patience for an example to those who were to believe in him for eternal life. To the King of ages, immortal, invisible, the only God, be honor and glory for ever and ever. (1 Timothy 1:15-17)

God alone—the only One worthy of honor and glory for what he has done and is doing in us—can cause us to live with this praise of him in our hearts.

CHAPTER 2

The Passion of Paul

The expression *passio Pauli*, "the passion of Paul," is commonly used to refer to the last part of the Acts of the Apostles, chapters 21 to 28, which describes the time from his imprisonment in Jerusalem to his imprisonment in Rome.

I would like to widen the meaning of the "passion of Paul" to include the other kinds of suffering that we know about, partly from allusions in his letters and partly from tradition. It is curious that Acts does not narrate the whole of Paul's life but stops at a certain point and then introduces the chapters on his "passion." His apostolic activity is described with the same number of chapters as those that describe his initial imprisonment, his trial, and finally his imprisonment in Rome.

Similarly in the gospels, the passion of Christ receives a lengthy treatment when compared to the brevity of the narration of his life that precedes it. The gospel writers cover two or three years of Christ's public life relatively briefly but describe the passion almost hour by hour, minute by minute. We can see from this the importance that the gospel writers and the early Church gave to the passion of Christ and to that of Paul.

The evangelists understood that Christ was the Messiah and the revealer of the Father, particularly in his passion. The same is true for Paul, who is a witness to Christ, not only in discourses that are passionate or erudite or full of gentleness, but also when he is a prisoner, is brought before courts, and is transferred from one jail to another—with his future uncertain, with serious limitations to his freedom, and with the threat of death.

In our reflection, let us proceed by answering these questions:

■ What are the similarities and differences between the passion of Christ and the passion of Paul?

■ What is the passion of a Christian?

■ How did Paul go through his passion?

■ How should we go through our passion?

Similarities and Differences

Let us look at some of the phases of Christ's passion in comparison to those of Paul, highlighting three events: Christ's arrest and Paul's arrest; Christ and Paul before the courts; and the physical and emotional sufferings of Christ and of Paul.

Christ's Arrest and Paul's Arrest

> While he was still speaking, there came a crowd, and the man called Judas, one of the twelve, was leading them. He drew near to Jesus to kiss him; but Jesus said to him, "Judas, would you betray the Son of man with a kiss?" And when those who were about him saw what would follow, they said, "Lord, shall we strike with the sword?" (Luke 22:47-49)

> When the seven days were almost completed, the Jews from Asia, who had seen him in the temple, stirred up all the crowd, and laid hands on him, crying out, "Men of Israel, help! This is the man who is teaching men everywhere against the people and the law and this place; moreover he also brought Greeks into the temple, and he has defiled this holy place." (Acts 21:27-28)

The whole city is in turmoil. Paul is dragged out of the temple; they close the gates, and they try to kill him. When the tribune arrives with the praetorian guard, they arrest him and bind him with two chains. From this moment on, Paul is in prison for a very long time.

What do these two scenes have in common, despite their differences? In both cases, the arrests are treacherous and unjust; they are underhanded ambushes. They are traps for both Jesus and Paul, skillfully set by their enemies.

The arrests come at a time when they are both giving themselves for their people. For Jesus, it happens during a night of prayer; for Paul, it comes at the moment of offering when, after having brought alms for his people, he humbly submits himself to being purified in the temple. The two events are connected in terms of their apostolic dedication, their service.

Christ and Paul before the Courts

Jesus appears before various courts: the Sanhedrin and Pilate's tribunal, an interrogation with a variety of accusations to which he responds at first, but at a certain point, becomes silent. Paul's trial is more fully described and is marked by a long series of discourses: his speech on the steps of the temple in chapter 22 of Acts; his speech before the Sanhedrin (chapter 23); his speech before Felix (chapter 24); his pleading before Festus (chapter 25); and the speech before King Agrippa (chapter 26). Paul gives a series of speeches in his defense, unlike Jesus who only speaks a few words.

It is interesting to note this difference in the two situations: Paul is not a slavish imitator of Jesus. He feels the Spirit of God within him, inspiring him to the life of the Master. He is handling his circumstances with appropriate responsibility, and he conducts himself with dignity, with resolution. He imitates Jesus in his dignity, in his sense of justice, in his nobility of soul. However, he acts differently in the thorough and vigorous manner with which he defends himself in his attempt to refute his adversaries. He succeeds in dividing the Sanhedrin by making his accusers argue among themselves.

By contrast, Jesus demonstrates his perseverance with very few words when he affirms his mission and boldly says, "You yourself say it; you say I am a king. You will see the Son of man at the right hand of the power of God" (see Matthew 26:64; Mark 14:62; Luke 22:69).

Behind an appearance of justice in both trials, we see that personal interests, fears, and conflicts from individual or group ambitions prevail. Both Jesus and Paul are subjected to the vicissitudes of human judgment. Even if Paul might have some hope—he always had hope in the letters in which he insisted on respect for authority—he learns that greedy and mean-spirited self-interest also prevails in those who should be upholding justice.

Physical and Emotional Sufferings

The sufferings of Christ seem much greater because they are fully described in the account of the passion. As for Paul, one can only intuit the oppressive situation of being in prison. He had already undergone considerable suffering in the scourgings and stonings to which he had been subjected. He refers to them almost as expected events.

Paul puts more emphasis on the emotional suffering, especially loneliness. This is the feature that most fully points to what unites our passion with the passion of Christ and of Paul.

Certainly the most grievous emotional suffering that Christ undergoes is due to his total abandonment by people. They all flee; only Peter follows him from afar, and then he denies him. Jesus, who was used to having support—an easy habit for us to form—finds himself quickly abandoned to intense loneliness. His loneliness is increased by the mysterious abandonment by God, which is expressed in his cry, "My God, my God, why hast thou forsaken me?" (Matthew 27:46). Much has been written to try to understand what this cry might mean.

The most dramatic and beautiful pages are perhaps those of Hans Urs von Balthasar in his *Mistero pasquale*.[1] Starting with Jesus' cry, he attempts to interpret Jesus' Good Friday: the darkness that crushes his soul and his descent into hell. Balthasar starts with the premise that we can interpret the passion of Jesus through the passion of the saints. Understanding the darkness, the desolation, the intense moments of abandonment that great saints have experienced, we can surmise something of what Jesus experienced first before the others, for the sake of all, to comfort and sustain all.

What can we say then of the emotional suffering of Paul?

Paul experienced his *passio* for a long time, even up to the end of his life: a progressive abandonment by his disciples. This man who is so full of energy makes statements that do not succeed in concealing that he is weary and feels he has suffered to the limit of his strength:

Do your best to come to me soon. [These are the words of someone who has really reached his limit.] For Demas, in love with this present world, has deserted me and gone to Thessalonica; Crescens has gone to Galatia, Titus to Dalmatia. [He is saying he is there almost all alone.] Luke alone is with me. Get Mark and bring him with you; for he is very useful in serving me. . . . Alexander the coppersmith did me great harm; the Lord will requite him for his deeds. Beware of him yourself, for he strongly opposed our message. At my first defense no one took my part; all deserted me. May it not be charged against them! (2 Timothy 4:9-11, 14-16)

This is a different Paul than the one we are used to knowing. He is physically weary, exhausted by prison, which is also obvious in the other "pastoral" letters to Timothy and Titus. It is not of interest for us to determine whether these writings are from his own hand or if they report his exact words. We accept them as the Church has transmitted them to us—as an expression of the character of the apostle the way the early Church knew him and conveyed him to us.

Certainly, the passage gives us the image of a Paul in a downward spiral. He is no longer the fervent author of the Letter to the Galatians or the Letter to the Romans with their great theological syntheses. This is a man who is struggling against daily difficulties and is lonely, and he lets a certain pessimism seep out. He denounces what is happening and foresees future evils; a dark and lamenting tone has taken the place of hope, boldness, and ardor.

This trial that Paul has gone through is a real trial. He recognizes that he is no longer in complete control of his strength, his optimism, his enthusiasm; he must now deal with weariness and an accumulation of burdens and disappointments. God wants to show us through him that a human being is purified in many ways, and this is a profound kind of purification.

We could ask if Paul experienced abandonment by God, internal darkness, desolation, the dark night of the soul. Autobiographically, it is impossible to determine one way or the other. However, he speaks over and over again about the hidden forces of evil that try to lure people into darkness, that attack people and show no mercy. He is familiar, then, with these powers of darkness that continuously attack the inner life of every human being.

Based on what Balthasar says about Jesus, we must conclude that Paul probably also experienced times when his faith was shrouded in darkness, and when he had to keep moving forward with only a memory of the abundance he possessed and the power of God that he no longer presently experienced.

The Passion of the Christian

I was struck some time ago by a book that describes the test of faith of Thérèse of Lisieux. The last part of this saint's life was profoundly dark. After receiving wonderful gifts from God, she entered into a state that is almost incomprehensible. She herself said it was a trial of the soul that could not be put into words, and she was almost afraid of speaking about it. The following are some significant passages from Thérèse's writings:

I imagine I was born in a country which is covered in thick fog. I never had the experience of contemplating the joyful appearance of nature flooded and transformed by the brilliance of the sun. . . . Then suddenly the fog which surrounds me becomes more dense; it penetrates my soul and envelops it in such a way that it is impossible to discover within it the sweet image of my Fatherland; everything has disappeared! When I want to rest my heart fatigued by the darkness which surrounds it by the memory of the luminous country after which I aspire, my torment redoubles; it seems to me that the darkness, borrowing the voice of sinners, says mockingly to me: "You are dreaming about the light, about a fatherland embalmed in the sweetest perfumes; you are dreaming about the *eternal* possession of the Creator of all these marvels; you believe that one day you will walk out of this fog which surrounds you! Advance, advance; rejoice in death which will give you not what you hope for but a night still more profound, the night of nothingness."[2]

When I sing of the happiness of heaven and of the eternal possession of God, I feel no joy in this, for I sing simply what I WANT TO BELIEVE. It is true that at times a very small ray of the sun comes to illumine my darkness, and then the trial ceases for *an instant,* but afterwards the memory of this ray, instead of causing me joy, makes my darkness even more dense.[3]

On the day of her death, September 30, 1897, she said she was experiencing pure agony without any trace of consolation.

These are striking words. Perhaps one of the harshest is a statement overheard by a nun that came to light during the process of beatification: "If you only knew what darkness I am plunged into. I don't believe in eternal life; I think that after this life there is nothing. Everything has disappeared on me, and I am left with love alone."[4]

She seems no longer to believe, but she believes that love exists. It is not a contradiction, it is the terrible purification of charity. These experiences are part of the Christian path.

We can also find confessions of this kind from other saints. St. Paul of the Cross, during his last illness, says some things that really make a person think. He confided to one of the brothers one day that he was feeling very violent impulses to escape into the woods and that he felt the urge to throw himself out of a window, which seem to be temptations to suicide. He was having very strong, uninterrupted temptations to despair.[5]

His despair is evident in a letter to a woman under his spiritual direction:

Ah! a soul that has experienced heavenly caresses and then finds it must for a time be deprived of everything; even more to come to a place where, as it seems to the soul, it is abandoned by God; where it seems God no longer wants it, does not care for it, and God seems to be highly displeased with it; when it seems that everything it has done has been done badly—ah! I do not know how to explain myself the way I would want. It is enough to know, my daughter, that this is almost a pain of the damned—I will say that—a pain which goes beyond every pain.[6]

Elsewhere he says,

The impression of having lost faith, hope, and charity, of feeling oneself lost in a tempestuous sea without anyone—from heaven or earth—offering a plank to escape drowning. There is no light from God; one is unable to think the smallest thought, unable to deal with any point about the spiritual life, feeling as desolate as the mountains of Gilboa and entombed in ice. In vocalized prayers I can do nothing except to get through the beads on the rosary.[7]

A brother reports that when he entered the room where Paul lay sick, he heard him cry out three times, in a voice that would move anyone to compassion, "I am abandoned!"

Certainly the character of a person comes into play here. Someone who is very sensitive can end up speaking this way about themselves during certain times of fatigue, depression, or illness. However, it is true that God mysteriously permits his saints to experience the trial of abandonment. It is a real experience, and when it occurs, we should recall that this is the experience of Christ on the cross, of Paul, of many saints.

Immediately after writing to Timothy that "all deserted me," Paul affirmed, however, "But the Lord stood by me and gave me strength. . . . The Lord will rescue me from every evil and save me for his heavenly kingdom. To him be the glory for ever and ever. Amen" (2 Timothy 4:17-18).

The power of the Spirit in him enabled him to overcome a moment in which he could have been tempted even to despair. We cannot know, though, if the last quarter hour of his life was a time of brightness and clarity or of darkness. The mystery of the human journey is always advancing toward the experience of death.

Precisely for this reason, we need to reflect about ourselves, about the sufferings others can go through, and about the need for knowing how to offer help. A sick person, especially a very sick person, opens up with great difficulty and perhaps only to someone he or she completely trusts. The task is to draw out this trust so as to provide help in the trials against faith and hope that a dying person can experience.

It is said that Thérèse of the Child Jesus remained susceptible toward the end of her life to an inexpressible agitation and anxiety that frightened the other nuns. They heard her say, "Pray for those who are sick and dying, little sisters. If you only knew what goes on!"[8] The lives of the saints can indeed help us to penetrate more deeply into the *passio Christi* and the *passio Pauli*.

Paul in Union with the Passion of Christ

From the letters in which Paul speaks of his sufferings, we understand first of all that God has given him the gift of going through them with a *great spirit of faith*, as he weighs their significance in the light of God's salvific plan.

> Our Savior Christ Jesus . . . appointed [me] a preacher and apostle and teacher, and therefore I suffer as I do. But I am not ashamed, for I know whom I have believed, and I am sure that he is able to guard until that Day what has been entrusted to me. (2 Timothy 1:9-12)

Paul's spirit of faith is saturated with an *ecclesial understanding* about what he is suffering:

> Remember Jesus Christ, risen from the dead, descended from David, as preached in my gospel, the gospel for which I am suffering and wearing fetters like a criminal. But the word of God is not fettered. Therefore I endure everything for the sake of the elect, that they also may obtain the salvation which in Christ Jesus goes with eternal glory. (2 Timothy 2:8-10)

It is as if he is saying, "I suffer, but it is for others, for the whole church, for the work of Christ":

> Now I rejoice in my sufferings for your sake, and in my flesh I complete what is lacking in Christ's afflictions for the sake of his body, that is, the church, of which I became a minister according to the divine office which was given to

me for you, to make the word of God fully known. (Colossians 1:24-25)

His profound sense of mission, which is the interior mainspring of all that he does for the church, does not abandon him, even in these times of crisis. Rather, it gives him the grace to consider these times as fully completing his service.

What About Our Passion?

We can conclude by asking ourselves about our attitude.

First of all, we must acknowledge that we are very weak and susceptible to being tempted, perhaps even in small things. We all have to go through these difficult times. A sense of our weakness is important because otherwise we risk speaking about these things in a facile way. When we actually find ourselves experiencing them, we can react in a completely different way, changing our whole way of viewing things. Being conscious of our weakness allows us to better connect what we read in Scripture with how we live.

This is why the vigilance I spoke about and which Paul himself mentions is necessary:

When people say, "There is peace and security," then sudden destruction will come upon them as travail comes upon a woman with child, and there will be no escape. But you are not in darkness, brethren, for that day to surprise you like a thief. For you are all sons of light and sons of the day; we are not of the night or of darkness. So then let us not sleep, as others do, but let us keep awake and be sober. (1 Thessalonians 5:3-6)

But, since we belong to the day, let us be sober, and put on the breastplate of faith and love, and for a helmet the hope of salvation. (1 Thessalonians 5:8)

Put on the whole armor of God, that you may be able to stand against the wiles of the devil. For we are not contending against flesh and blood, but against the principalities, against the powers, against the world rulers of this present darkness, against the spiritual hosts of wickedness in the heavenly places. Therefore take the whole armor of God, that you may be able to withstand in the evil day, and having done all, to stand. (Ephesians 6:11-13)

Christian life presents us with a test that is no light matter because it pits us against an implacable enemy who returns again and again to attack us. When we think of daily life, the simple everyday things, this kind of talk may seem excessive. But if we delve more deeply into our lives and the lives of other people, if we consider the very sad trials that people experience and the problems that lead to anxiety and despair, then we see more clearly that the enemy of the human race is at work. He tries, through all the simplest, most hidden, and most subtle ways, to make each of us lose our faith and hope, offering us a life of resignation without the context of God's plan of salvation to give it any meaning. He continuously wants to destroy the spark of faith that allows us to see everything as God's work in us and as our path toward him.

The New Testament exhorts us to be vigilant and to resist because its authors were very familiar with the human condition and knew that trials will come to everyone. When we think that the trials are behind us, in reality they are closer than ever.

Let us ask the Lord in our contemplation of the passion of Christ and of the passion of Paul that we may walk in the way of God and may stand upright, that we may resist all difficulties with courage, and that we may help others, many others, lest they succumb to the trial.

1. Hans Urs von Balthasar, *Mistero pasquale: The Mystery of Easter*, trans. by Aidan Nichols (Edinburgh: Clark, 1990), 76–79.

2. Thérèse of Lisieux, *The Story of a Soul: The Autobiography of St. Thérèse of Lisieux*, trans. John Clark (Washington, DC: ICS Publications, 1972), 212–213.

3. Thérèse of Lisieux, 214.

4. Thérèse of Lisieux, *St. Thérèse of Lisieux by Those Who Knew Her*, ed. and trans. Christopher O'Mahony (Huntington, IN: Our Sunday Visitor, 1975), 195.

5. Charles Alméras, *St. Paul of the Cross, Founder of the Passionists*, trans. M. Angeline Bouchard (Garden City, NY: Hanover House, 1960), 95.

6. Letter to Agnes Grazi, Oct. 3, 1736, in *The Letters of Saint Paul of the Cross*, vol. 1, ed. Laurence Finn and Donald Webber, trans. Roger Mercurio and Frederick Sucher (Hyde Park, NY: New City Press, 2000), 148.

7. See Alméras, 94–96, for similar examples.

8. Thérèse of Lisieux, *The Story of a Soul*, 265.

CHAPTER 3

Paul's Transfiguration

Proceeding from the historical events of the suffering in Paul's life, let us reflect on the transfiguration that his inner purification led to in order to meditate on our own transfiguration.

Our point of reference is the transfiguration of Christ: "And as he was praying, the appearance of his countenance was altered, and his raiment became dazzling white" (Luke 9:29). It is interesting to note that the word "dazzling" used here has the same root as the word Luke uses in Acts 9 to describe the light Paul enters during his vision in Damascus: Paul is experiencing the reflection of the transfigured Christ.

When describing the scene of Jesus' transfiguration, Mark's gospel speaks of transformation: "he was transformed; he was transfigured" (see Mark 9:2). The Greek verb *metamorphothē* ("he was transformed") is translated this way in Mark: "and he was transfigured before them, and his garments became glistening, intensely white" (9:2-3). *Metamorphothē* is the same word that Paul uses in his Letter to the Corinthians to describe the process of transformation that he, and every apostle and pastor after him, experiences in reflecting the glory of Christ:

And we all [it is clear that he is describing an experience he wants us to share], with unveiled face, beholding the glory of the Lord [or "reflecting like mirrors the brightness of the Lord"], are being changed [transfigured or transformed] into his likeness from one degree of glory to another; for this comes from the Lord who is the Spirit. (2 Corinthians 3:18)

Paul, enveloped by the glory of the Lord at Damascus, is being transformed. But the verb is in the present tense to indicate an ongoing transformation, from glory to glory, through the power of the Spirit of God. He is being transformed into the image of Jesus, he is acquiring the brightness of Christ.

Let us not forget that the event of Christ's transfiguration is widely used in the liturgy of the Greek church to refer to what happens to Christians through the progressive integration of their baptismal gifts.

In speaking of the "transfiguration" of Paul, I am referring to the increasing brightness and transparency that occurs in him during his pastoral career and that is reflected in an unsurpassing way in his major letters.

Reading those letters, we are drawn by the clarity and the splendor of his soul; even after two thousand years we can still sense behind the written words a living, breathing, dynamic, and inspiring person.

His transfigured personality attracted people and constituted one of the secrets of his apostolic work. It was the result of a long journey of trial, suffering, incessant prayer, and renewed confidence.

Let us try to analyze his character, since that can give us a perfect mirror with which to compare ourselves.

■ What are the characteristics of the luminosity in Paul? We can derive them from three inner attitudes that are typical of this kind of transfiguration and from two of his modes of action.

■ And next, how do we attain and maintain in ourselves something similar to this transfiguration, which is a gift from God for us as well?

Paul's Inner Attitudes

The first attitude we find in all his letters, even in the ones where Paul is engaged in conflict, is a *great inner joy and peace*: "I am filled with comfort. With all our affliction, I am overjoyed" (2 Corinthians 7:4). Paul clearly links his many tribulations with joy, even an overflowing joy. We can tell from this same letter that his joy is not forced or idealistic: "[W]e have this treasure in earthen vessels, to show that the transcendent power belongs to God and not to us" (2 Corinthians 4:7). Paul recognizes that this extraordinary joy comes from God; he could not possess it on his own. This is typical of transfiguration: it is not merely the fruit of good character; it is not merely a natural, human gift.

We are afflicted in every way, but not crushed; perplexed, but not driven to despair; persecuted, but not forsaken; struck down, but not destroyed; always carrying in the body the death of Jesus, so that the life of Jesus may also be manifested in our bodies. (2 Corinthians 4:8-10)

This is not mere tranquility; it is a true joy that deals with every kind of burden, difficulty, and unpleasant thing that happens to him, with the misunderstandings and the ups and downs that he faces in daily life—the same kinds of things we experience. Paul was a bit melancholic in temperament, and because of that he was subject to depression and times of discouragement. He gradually realizes during his life, though, that in every instance of discouragement, something much stronger rises up in him.

In addition, it is a joy that is outwardly oriented; it is for his community, not merely for him. It is joy for what is happening around him, for the community that is following him: "We work with you for your joy" (2 Corinthians 1:24). Writing to the Philippians, he defines their community as "my joy and crown" (4:1). Let us not deceive ourselves that this was an ideal, perfect community. From that same letter to the Philippians we know that Paul had to plead with them, almost on bended knee, to not quarrel, to not speak against one another, to not be divided. "Do nothing from selfishness or conceit" (2:3). This means that selfishness and conceit existed there, that the community was not an easy one, and that it caused problems and irritations for him. And yet, he succeeded in considering it his joy, because he was given a vision of faith that goes beyond purely pragmatic and routine considerations. His joy was a genuine supernatural gift, a strengthening from the Spirit that was present in him to a remarkable degree by that time.

The second inner attitude, which follows from the first, is Paul's *capacity for gratitude*. He exhorted his people to thank the Father with joy (see Colossians 1:11-12). It is typical of the apostle to combine joy with thanksgiving.

All his letters begin with a prayer of thanksgiving (except for the one to the Galatians because it is a letter of correction). Paul knows how to give thanks, and his words do not come from an empty formula but express what he feels. Furthermore, the New Testament itself begins with a prayer of thanksgiving. The earliest written section of the New Testament, the one that in all probability preceded even the final version of the gospels, is the First Letter to the Thessalonians. Therefore, probably the first words of the New Testament to be written were "Grace to you and peace. We give thanks to God always for you all" (1 Thessalonians 1:1-2).

On the other hand, we never find unproductive disapproval in Paul. We find reproof but not a resigned bitterness. As a gift of God, through his apostolic transfiguration, he has the capacity always to see the good first. Beginning every letter with thanks means that he knows how to value primarily the positive in whatever community he is writing to, even if there are some weighty, negative things that will need to be said.

At the beginning of the First Letter to the Corinthians the community is praised for being filled with every spiritual gift and all knowledge. Then the reproofs come, but this is not incongruous. The eyes of faith enable him to see that the spark of faith in his poor pagan converts is such an immense gift that he praises God incessantly for it.

The mature pastor has the ability to recognize the good that is present and to express it with simplicity.

The third attitude is *praise*. We find in Paul those marvelous praises that continue the Jewish tradition of blessings. He knows how to expand them to encompass everything that concerns the life of the community in Christ. For example, "Blessed be the God and Father of our Lord Jesus Christ, who has blessed us in Christ with every spiritual blessing in the heavenly places" (Ephesians 1:3). Paul's prayer, as we know from his letters, consists first of all of praise. It also moves on into intercession, but his first spontaneous expression is praise. This is how he makes the most of his darkest moments:

Blessed be the God and Father of our Lord Jesus Christ, the Father of mercies and God of all comfort, who comforts us in all our affliction, so that we may be able to comfort those who are in any affliction, with the comfort with which we ourselves are comforted by God. (2 Corinthians 1:3-4)

The grace that we need to ask God for is that these attitudes become our habitual experience. The devil continually tempts us to fall back into worldly ways of life: sadness characterizes people whose prospects seem closed, and deep-seated sadness seeks for escape, for entertainment, for distraction—anything that seems to make life cheerful in order to avoid facing the sadness.

Paul's Modes of Action

The first mode of action that points to Paul's transformation involves *a never-ending capacity to bounce back* that is truly astounding.

From the very first day of his conversion, he preaches at Damascus and has to flee. He goes to Jerusalem, he preaches, and they make him leave. He remains in Tarsus until Providence calls him back. When he is called back, bad feelings from the past are forgotten, and he leaves again. In his missionary journey, practically every stop requires starting all over from the beginning. He preaches in Antioch of Pisida, is chased out, and goes to Iconium. Some people in Iconium organize a plot against him and try to stone him, so he goes to Lystra. In Lystra he is subjected to a hail of stones. It is interesting to note the lack of emotion with which Luke describes the situation:

> But Jews came there from Antioch and Iconium; and having persuaded the people, they stoned Paul and dragged him out of the city, supposing that he was dead. But when the disciples gathered about him, he rose up and entered the city; and on the next day he went on with Barnabas to Derbe. When they had preached the gospel to that city and had made many disciples, they returned to Lystra and to Iconium and to Antioch. (Acts 14:19-21)

This is in some ways the pattern of his life. He leaves Athens humiliated, mocked by the philosophers, yet he goes to Corinth and starts all over again, even if he is filled with dread.

This ability to bounce back is more than human; anyone, after so many failed attempts, would be humanly unnerved. We do not possess this tirelessness; even he did not possess it. It is a manifestation of what he will call "charity" or "love": "Love . . . endures all things" (1 Corinthians 13:7). It is the love of God: "God's love has been poured into our hearts through the Holy Spirit who has been given to us" (Romans 5:5). Paul's behavior here comes from above; it is a gift that ensures that disappointment can never be definitive:

> More than that, we rejoice in our sufferings, knowing that suffering produces endurance, and endurance produces character, and character produces hope, and hope does not disappoint us, because God's love has been poured into our hearts through the Holy Spirit who has been given to us. (Romans 5:3-5)

If these words were spoken by a new convert in the initial stages of enthusiasm, we could think that he or she was speaking naïvely. However, being spoken by a missionary after twenty years of trials, these words take on a different character and cause us to reflect deeply. No human effort can achieve this attitude. It comes from the love of God poured into our hearts through the Spirit who has been given to us.

This transfiguration of Paul occurs, once more, through the power of the risen One who enters into Paul's weakness and lives in him.

The second mode of action is characterized by *freedom in the spirit*. He knows that he has reached a place in which he no longer acts through pressure or conformity to external standards. He acts out of his inner abundance. He is truly able, consequently, to take on fervent attitudes that would otherwise be reckless for him to try to imitate.

We see this freedom in the spirit in the Letter to the Galatians when he says that, humanly speaking, it would have been more prudent to circumcise Titus according to the demands of the Jewish Christians. However, Paul notes, "To them we did not yield submission even for a moment, that the truth of the gospel might be preserved for you" (Galatians 2:5).

Paul is free from every current of popular opinion. It is very difficult to remain isolated in the face of a common mentality and an opposing culture. Nevertheless, he does so with complete liberty, and without feeling sorry for himself, because the weight of others' opinions cannot compare to the inner abundance he feels. This inner strength permits him at a certain point to oppose even Cephas in dealing with an ultimate case of freedom: "And with him [Peter in Antioch] the rest of the Jews acted insincerely, so that even Barnabas was carried away by their insincerity" (Galatians 2:13). What he calls insincerity on the part of Barnabas was evidently his desire to mediate between the parties. Paul does not accept that, and it is his resistance that ends up clarifying the situation.

This freedom is not arbitrary or presumptuous but rather comes from a sense of absolute and total belonging to Christ as a slave, as a servant. He sometimes makes the parallel between being a servant of Christ and being free of all human opinions.

In this light, freedom becomes the most rigorous form of service:

For freedom Christ has set us free; stand fast therefore, and do not submit again to a yoke of slavery.

Now I, Paul, say to you that if you receive circumcision, Christ will be of no advantage to you. I testify again to every man who receives circumcision that he is bound to keep the whole law. You are severed from Christ, you who would be justified by the law; you have fallen away from grace. For through the Spirit, by faith, we wait for the hope of righteousness. For in Christ Jesus neither circumcision nor uncircumcision is of any avail, but faith working through love. You were running well; who hindered you from obeying the truth? This persuasion is not from him who called you. A little leaven leavens the whole lump. I have confidence in the Lord that you will take no other view than mine; and he who is troubling you will bear his judgment, whoever he is. But if I, brethren, still preach circumcision, why am I still persecuted? In that case the stumbling block of the cross has been removed. I wish those who unsettle you would mutilate themselves!

For you were called to freedom, brethren; only do not use your freedom as an opportunity for the flesh, but through love be servants of one another. (Galatians 5:1-13)

This is one of the few passages in which being a servant—in Greek, "being a slave"—is applied to how Christians should act with one another. The absolute nature of service to Christ makes a person so free that he or she is not afraid of being the slave of another brother or sister. This freedom, then, is the source of the humblest service and is the root of an approach "with all humility" (Acts 20:19) that characterizes Paul's apostolate.

It is difficult to express these things in words, because if they are analyzed in detail, they can sound commonplace. The effort, however, can serve as an invitation to reread Paul's texts and to let his inspired words act on us with all their power.

Our Transfiguration

I would like to reflect on the way to attain and maintain our own transfiguration. Paul begins to become a pastor according to Christ's heart after fifteen years of hard work and suffering. This occurs through God's gift and not through his own achievement. The fundamental path to transfiguration is to recognize that it is God who, in his mercy, transfigures us.

The first way of receiving this divine gift is a *contemplation of the heart of the crucified Christ* that pours out the Spirit. We could call this eucharistic contemplation: to take seriously the twofold meal of the word of God and of the Eucharist, to allow ourselves to be nourished by the word of God as the power that reveals the historical, salvific meaning of the meal that is Christ crucified and risen. This meal becomes our nourishment and inserts us into the story of salvation, whose reality, magnitude, and orientation is imparted by the word of God. As it was for Paul, this contemplation is the path to transfiguration for us, as well. The apostle lived the continual and enduring prayer that consists of the contemplation of Christ crucified and risen.

The gift of a heart transfigured in joy, in praise, in thanksgiving, in perseverance, and in freedom comes through the *intercession of Mary*. As a mystery of God in the history of the Church and of salvation, it is she who sustains and nourishes the liveliness of faith in us. A mature Christian can discover the role of the Virgin as a model and intercessor in acquiring humble dependence on the word of God, which transfigures us and ensures continued openness to the renewing power of the Spirit. Mary calls us to live authentically the kind of contemplation and listening that characterizes her role in the Church.

The gift of transfiguration also comes from *sharing*, from stretching out a hand in the dark and placing it on the shoulder of someone who sees the light. This is our ecclesial communion: to place a hand on the shoulder of someone who has seen the light and to do that for each other. This is the role of spiritual direction or of conversations in the confessional that are so important because they involve extending hands to one another. They are practical ways of opening ourselves and of maintaining the gifts that we admire in Paul that come from transfiguration.

The gift of transfiguration needs evangelical *vigilance*. "Watch and pray that you may not enter into temptation; the spirit indeed is willing, but the flesh is weak" (Matthew 26:41; Mark 14:38); "Be watchful, stand firm in your faith" (1 Corinthians 16:13). This repeated invitation is an exhortation based on the fundamental insight that human beings are limited creatures who grow weary and who are not capable of persevering on their own. Every Christian, every bishop, and every priest needs to be convinced that no one is assured of persevering; those who think they have reached a certain stage of stability in which precautions are no longer necessary are at great risk. New Testament vigilance instructs us that until the hour of our death, the devil tries to take our joy, faith, and praise. We are always attacked regarding these fundamental attitudes. We need to be vigilant, knowing that there is no truce in this battle and that we can quickly find ourselves sad, weary, nervous, irritated, or even dissipated in external joys that weaken our faith. Paul often returns to the themes of vigilance and of insistence on prayer.

Let us ask Mary for her intercession to be able to watch with her, with Jesus, and with Paul so that the transfiguration may be accomplished in us, the transfiguration that—despite difficulties, suffering, and disappointments—assures us a life in which our innermost selves are possessed by Christ and firmly held in God's hands.

PART II

APOSTLE BY VOCATION

Chapter 4

The Mystery of the Church

A Reading from Ephesians 5:1-33:

[1]Therefore be imitators of God, as beloved children. [2]And walk in love, as Christ loved us and gave himself up for us, a fragrant offering and sacrifice to God.

[3]But immorality and all impurity or covetousness must not even be named among you, as is fitting among saints. [4]Let there be no filthiness, nor silly talk, nor levity, which are not fitting; but instead let there be thanksgiving. [5]Be sure of this, that no immoral or impure man, or one who is covetous (that is, an idolater), has any inheritance in the kingdom of Christ and of God. [6]Let no one deceive you with empty words, for it is because of these things that the wrath of God comes upon the sons of disobedience. [7]Therefore do not associate with them, [8]for once you were darkness, but now you are light in the Lord; walk as children of light [9](for the fruit of light is found in all that is good and right and true), [10]and try to learn what is pleasing to the Lord. [11]Take no part in the unfruitful works of darkness, but instead expose them. [12]For it is a shame even to speak of the things that they do in secret; [13]but when anything is exposed by the light it becomes visible, for anything that become visible is light. [14]Therefore it is said,

"Awake, O sleeper, and arise from the dead,
and Christ shall give you light."

[15]Look carefully then how you walk, not as unwise men but as wise, [16]making the most of the time, because the days are evil. [17]Therefore do not be foolish, but understand what the will of the Lord is. [18]And do not get drunk with wine, for that is debauchery; but be filled with the Spirit, [19]addressing one another in psalms and hymns and spiritual songs, singing and making melody to the Lord with all your heart, [20]always and for everything giving thanks in the name of our Lord Jesus Christ to God the Father.

[21]Be subject to one another out of reverence for Christ. [22]Wives, be subject to your husbands, as to the Lord. [23]For the husband is the head of the wife as Christ is the head of the church, his body, and is himself its Savior. [24]As the church is subject to Christ, so let wives also be subject in everything to their husbands. [25]Husbands, love your wives, as Christ loved the church and gave himself up for her, [26]that he might sanctify her, having cleansed her by the washing of water with the word, [27]that he might present the church to himself in splendor, without spot or wrinkle or any such thing, that she might be holy and without blemish. [28]Even so husbands should love their wives as their own bodies. He who loves his wife loves himself. [29]For no man ever hates his own flesh, but nourishes and cherishes it, as Christ does the church, [30]because we are members of his body. [31]"For this reason a man shall leave his father and mother and be joined to his wife, and the two shall become one." [32]This is a great mystery, and I mean in reference to Christ and the church; [33]however, let each one of you love his wife as himself, and let the wife see that she respects her husband.

The General Context

Chapter 5 is part of the concluding section of the Letter to the Ephesians in which the apostle pauses to discuss the new life in Christ. After giving some general information about this new life, Paul goes on to deal with domestic conduct, beginning with verse 21, and presents the ethical ideal for relationships between wife and husband, children and parents, and slaves and masters.

The teaching coincides, on the one hand, with the moral understanding current at the time. On the other hand, it is highly innovative, because it integrates everything with people's relationship with Christ.

To prove that, we only need to point out that the name "Christ" is repeated six times and is substituted once by "Lord" in this text on marital relations:

> Be subject to one another out of reverence for *Christ*. Wives, be subject to your husbands, as to the *Lord*. . . . *Christ* is the head of the church. . . . The church is subject to *Christ*. . . . *Christ* loved the church. . . . *Christ* [nourishes] the church. . . . [This is] in reference to *Christ* and the church.

Family conduct is thus reinterpreted in the light of its relation to the mystery of Christ.

The Dynamic in the Passage

The dynamic in the passage is also interesting. It begins with a general principle: submission "to one another out of reverence for Christ" (verse 21). Next, there is an application of that principle for wives (verses 22-24) and one for husbands (verses 25-28).

Then a provisional conclusion speaks about the necessity of caring for the wife (verses 29-30). Finally, the general conclusion ends the section, with an emphasis on the mystery:

> "For this reason a man shall leave his father and mother and be joined to his wife, and the two shall become one." This is a great mystery, and I mean in reference to Christ and the church; however, let each one of you love his wife as himself, and let the wife see that she respects her husband. (verses 31-33)

We get the impression that when speaking of the first covenant in human history—between husband and wife, the most fundamental of all covenants—Paul wants to bring it back to its deep root, the root that explains everything and from which everything derives: the covenant between Christ and the Church.

Christological Affirmations

I would like to point out the features of the Christ-church relationship through seven christological affirmations:

1. "Christ is the head of the church" (verse 23b).
2. Christ is the "Savior" of the "body" of the Church (verse 23c).
3. "Christ loved the church and gave himself up for her" (verse 25b).
4. He gave himself "that he might sanctify her, having cleansed her by the washing of water [baptism] with the word [the profession of faith]" (verse 26).
5. He did this so that "he might present the church to himself

[the image of baptism probably gives way to a wedding] in splendor, without spot or wrinkle or any such thing, that she might be holy and without blemish" (verse 27).

These five christological proclamations tell us how much Christ loves the Church, what he desires of her, and what his purpose is in giving himself completely in life and death.

Two other affirmations follow:

6. Christ "nourishes and cherishes" the Church (verse 29). In the metaphor of nourishment, we can see the theme of the Eucharist.

7. The last christological statement applies the "one flesh" of Genesis 2:24 to "Christ and the church" (verse 32).

It seems clear that the apostle is bringing the fundamental covenant between man and woman back to the primordial one that sheds light on everything else: the mystery of the unity between Christ and the Church.

What is the message in the text that helps us understand what love for the church means? It is a message that concerns the activity of Christ toward the church: Christ is the head, the savior, the nourisher.

He is the head, not only because he is Lord over the church, but also because he exercises his leadership as if he is the center of a wheel, coordinating her development so that she may grow into the fullness of charity. His function as head is described earlier in Ephesians 4:15-16:

Speaking the truth in love, we are to grow up in every way into him who is the head, into Christ, from whom the whole body, joined and knit together by every joint with which it is supplied, when each part is working properly, makes bodily growth and upbuilds itself in love.

The mention of Christ as the head of the Church in Ephesians 5:23 is related to this prior explanation in chapter 4.

A second function pinpoints the active role of Christ: "He is the Savior" (verse 23). Further ahead, in verses 25-27, he clarifies how Christ became the savior of the Church and how he continues his work of setting her free. It is a kind of kerygmatic synthesis of the process of salvation history that makes the Christ-Church relationship a kind of parable or symbolic prototype of Christian marriage. The vocabulary and the structure of the verses make us think of a Christian hymn or a passage of catechesis drawn from a traditional confession of faith.

Essentially, Paul is saying that the love of Christ for the church is at the origin of the process of salvation, the process that makes the Church a spouse who is "holy and without blemish" (verse 27). His love is demonstrated by giving himself completely for her.

The effects of his self-giving described in verses 26-27 recall baptism first of all, but in Paul's thinking they perhaps also include, among other things, the church's final appearance, perfect and complete before her Spouse.

The fundamental meaning of the passage is very clear: Christ has so loved the Church that he purifies her, he sanctifies her, and he nourishes her. His love is altruistic and not for his own gratification. He helps her to become beautiful, good, and perfect. All his activity is focused on her.

The Church is regarded by Paul as a spouse who is so well loved by her Lord, so well cared for, nourished, and adorned, that she is splendid. He sees the man and the woman who emerge from the baptismal font clothed with the glory and the love of Christ. Nevertheless, as I said earlier, he is thinking of the Church in her fullness, the fruit of the selfless love of Jesus—a Church that is washed and purified, the Church in her final condition, the heavenly Jerusalem, presented with the beauty of a bride that we see in the Song of Songs (see 4:7), the Church sanctified, chosen, and consecrated.

This text, though, raises questions and problems. What does it mean to proclaim the beauty of the Church when our historical experience of her is so different? The very lofty theological truth expressed by Paul contrasts with our daily experience. In what way, then, does Christ love not only the ideal Church but also the actual church the way she is? And how do we relate the historical Church to Christ's plan?

Before answering and as a way of entering into the *meditatio*, I will quote from a treatise on the Church by a German author:

The churches themselves always draw the public's attention. They are exposed to the gaze of public opinion, a gaze that scrutinizes mercilessly. They do not freely offer themselves to that gaze and would prefer to evade it, since what is seen in them is completely other than what should appear. And all that "appears" in the churches—cowardice, authoritarian attitudes, hypocrisy, narrow-mindedness— then gets ascribed in some way by public opinion to the God for whom these (Christian) churches exist. What appears in these churches as a rule does not speak on behalf of "their" God, a God who—as they maintain—is a God who loves people, a God whose heart is set on people and their salvation. It is precisely the churches that no longer make faith in God credible, at least the God of Jesus Christ and the Christians. If one must follow what is seen in those who try to live this faith in this God, then one cannot ascribe to the God of the Christians any possibility of finding faith among human beings in the future.[1]

Even though he speaks in a harsh and excessive tone, the real issue is clearly exposed.

I would like to reflect with you and try to pick out concrete patterns or approaches by which we arrive at love or disaffection for the Church. What are the means, the stages, by which the Church finally comes to be understood the way Jesus wants?

Approaches to Love and Disaffection for the Church

An Approach with Different Stages

In youth (I am thinking of my experience), people struggle to relate peacefully to an institution. Despite living and breathing in it, they do not succeed in feeling that it is their home, because they have their own subjectivity, their own dreams, their own moods, and their own ideals. They primarily see all the ways in which the historical Church falls short of her ideals, and they distance themselves.

People begin to relate to the Church more maturely in three stages.

First, we begin to understand that all that we are, all the good that we have and that represents our high moral and spiritual ideals, comes to us from the Church and not from our own efforts.

However, a *second* stage is needed that consists in understanding, at least theoretically, the value and the necessity of institutions and their capacity for continuity and duration. Personally, I came to understand rather late that institutions are precisely the things that "remain" compared to the tenuousness of the decisions and choices of individuals. At this point, a person's relationship to the Church becomes more real, more appropriate, more authentic.

There is finally a *third* stage that occurs in this process. When people invest something of value in the Church, they participate in the Church and suffer for her. To the extent that I not only receive from but also give to the Church, the circle completes itself, and the relationship becomes mature, balanced, and peaceful. However, this is still not the maturity that comes from a relationship of faith. In fact, this initial approach and its stages also apply to a person's relationship to civil institutions (the state, society).

A Spiritual Approach

The maturing of faith, genuine love for the Church, is birthed from love for Christ. In the passage from Ephesians cited above, Paul clearly affirms that. If we love Christ, we enter into his thoughts, and we realize how he "loved the church and gave himself up for her" (Ephesians 5:25).

It is from the heart of Christ that we contemplate the church as *Sponsa Verbi, creatura Verbi* (the spouse of the Word, the creation of the Word), a creation of the Spirit. A worldly interpretation of the Church will always be very imperfect and often disappointing, because it is not able to see the depths in her that come from the Lord.

I would like to quote a personal notation from Pope Paul VI's diary on this point:

The church—to love her, to serve her, to bear with her, and to build her up with all of one's ability, with all dedication, and with tireless patience and humility. This is what continually remains to be done, again and again, until everything is consummated, until everything is achieved (will it ever happen?), until he returns again. *In omnia fiducia sicut semper*, "with full courage now as always."[2]

This is a good paraphrase of the passage from the Letter to the Ephesians. Paul VI understood Jesus' gift of himself to the Church and therefore lived his own relationship with the Church in giving to, bearing with, building up, and serving her, dedicating all his abilities to that endeavor with tireless patience and humility.

Something else needs to be emphasized. People love the Church in a spirit of faith when they understand the similarity between the dialectical process of coming to know God and the dialectical process of understanding the Church. In both cases, it is a process of maintaining the tension between the visible and invisible, between blemishes and wrinkles and interior purity, between failures and glory. The dialectic through which we come to know God is the same, at least by analogy, as the one by which we arrive at a faith understanding of the Church.

I will try to clarify this idea, because I believe it is important.

We sense, on the one hand, that God is transcendent, elusive, unattainable—and always beyond our verification. On the other hand, we sense that God is immanent and makes himself present, even if he does so in unobtrusive, inviting, and gentle ways that are not scientifically provable.

Through simple signs, we see God in ourselves, in our lives, in the life of Christ. They are signs that people could be dubious about if they do not want to trust them or if they do not want to make an act of surrender, even though they know that such an act is reasonable. They are signs—as Luther called them—*sub contrario specie* (under a contradictory form): the servant of Yahweh whom we dare not look upon, the defeat of the cross.

We understand by faith that if God exists, he can only present himself as one who is elusive and yet who manifests himself, even if the signs are not obvious and are sometimes provocative or contradictory, like suffering, incapacity, and weakness. It is then that we discover that the Church can be understood through a parallel process.

The Church, the body of Christ, the spouse of Christ, the creation of the Spirit, is immensely loved by God and enriched with gifts that are manifested in history, but at the same time, it is marked by burdens, wrinkles, and sins, starting with those that each of us commits. We need to go beyond all the signs to arrive at the reality. Some of the signs must be superseded by thinking of their opposites (i.e., the defeat of the cross is actually victory), but some signs, from the perspective of faith, indicate our participation in the splendor of Christ.

There are endless numbers of both kinds of these signs. We can see a reflection of the splendor of Christ in the saints, but we can see in the historical unfaithfulness of the sons of the Church the painful failure that Jesus experienced with his apostles and that he carried with him to the cross.

Therefore, to love the Church, to understand her mystery with the fullness of Paul's understanding in the Letter to the Ephesians, we need to have a strong faith, a continuous orientation toward the world beyond, a capacity to contemplate the relationship between invisible realities and this world. Without the dynamic of faith, it will always be very easy to see only the ambiguity of the signs about the Church and then fail to see anything at all.

As an example of a faith-filled understanding of the mystery of the Church, I would like to quote Paul VI again, who asked, in the years after the Council,

> Does the church suffer today? Children, dearest children! Yes, today the church is enduring a trial of great sufferings! But why? Even after the Council? Yes, after the Council. The Lord is testing us. The church is suffering, as you know, from the oppressive lack of real freedom in so many countries of the world. She suffers from the abandonment by so many Catholics of their loyalty, which her centuries-old tradition should merit and which her pastoral effort, full of understanding and love, should obtain. She suffers most of all from the restless, critical, intractable, and destructive rebellion of so many of her children, her most beloved— priests, teachers, and lay people dedicated to the service and testimony of the living Christ in a church that is alive. The rebellion is against her intimate and vital communion, against her institutional existence, against her canonical norms, her tradition, her internal organization. . . . Dearest children, do not cast aside your spiritual solidarity and your prayer. Do not let yourselves be captured by fear, discouragement, skepticism. . . . Rather, suffer and love with the church; work and hope with the church.[3]

These words demonstrate the profound faith of a person who sees the sufferings, the weaknesses, the efforts, the blemishes of the Church, and yet sees in her the mystery of Christ; thus, he does not cease to give, to suffer, and to hope.

I ask myself how all this relates specifically to ministry. What does ministry add to the perspective of faith and to the dialectical process of knowing God and the Church that is valuable for every believer?

Certainly ministry reflects a very particular form of personal involvement with the reality of the Church. Whoever lives a life of ministry is involved professionally and can therefore know her better both in her efforts and in her weaknesses and can understand better how Christ loved her.

However, ministry, which brings a person into contact with the blemishes and wrinkles of the church beginning with his or her own, can be the source of many disappointments regarding the spouse of Christ in her historical journey.

Still, ministry fosters identification with Jesus that makes us participants of his benevolent love toward the Church. I love her because—and in the way that—Jesus loves her. I love her in order to help her become more and more as Jesus desires and sees her.

I will let Paul VI have the last word from his *Pensiero alla morte*:

> I ask the Lord . . . for the grace to make my approaching death a gift to the church. I can say that I have always loved her. It was love for her that drew me out of my petty, uncontrolled egotism and began me in her service. I seem to have lived because of her, and not anything else. But I would like the church to know it, and I would like the strength to say it, as a secret from the heart that a person has the courage to share only in the last moments of life.[4]

Let us also ask to have and express from our hearts this way of seeing and loving the Church, this way that enlightens us, that integrates us internally and brightens a path that is often difficult.

1. Jürgen Werbick, *Kirche: Ein Ekklesiologischer Entwurf für Studium und Praxis* [Church: An Ecclesiological Outline for Study and Praxis] (Freiburg: Herder, 1994), p. 25.

2. See Philippians 1:20 as the source and for the context of this phrase.

3. Pope Paul VI, General Audience, April 2, 1969.

4. Pope Paul VI, *Pensiero alla morte; Testamento; Omelia nel XV anniversario dell'incoronazione* [Thoughts on Death; Testament; Homily on the 15th Anniversary of His Papacy] (Brescia: Istituto Paolo VI, 1988), pp. 28-29.

CHAPTER 5

Love for the Community

A Reading from 2 Corinthians 3:1-3

[1]Are we beginning to commend ourselves again? Or do we need, as some do, letters of recommendation to you, or from you? [2]You yourselves are our letter of recommendation, written on [our] hearts, to be known and read by all men; [3]and you show that you are a letter from Christ delivered by us, written not with ink but with the Spirit of the living God, not on tablets of stone but on tablets of human hearts.

The Verses in Their Context

What are these verses from Paul saying in their immediate context? This is the first question for our *lectio*.

The context of the Second Letter to the Corinthians is that Paul is defending himself from the accusations of double-mindedness, insincerity, and trickery with which the community had sharply and rudely challenged him. He wants to explain himself, and he does so in a passionate tone typical of a person who has been unjustly treated.

Given that context, let us reread and analyze the first three verses of chapter 3.

First, Paul retorts to the accusations that wounded him deeply: others ought to have a letter of recommendation, not I (verse 1).

Immediately after, he uses the intriguing metaphor of a letter, which comes to mind now in a different way, precisely because of their attack: "You yourselves are our letter of recommendation, written on [our] hearts, to be known and read by all men; and you show that you are a letter from Christ delivered by us, written not with ink but with the Spirit of the living God, not on tablets of stone but on tablets of human hearts" (verses 2-3). These are positive and extraordinarily effective words that come from the apostle's heart—a suffering and impassioned heart—in a swirl of metaphors, negations, and affirmations.

"You yourselves are our letter of recommendation" is the central proclamation. In other words, "You are the most beautiful letter I have ever written, and I assure you I am proud of you." He is thus very aware of the gift of God and of its fruits. He has in fact written some very beautiful letters: the First and perhaps the Second (if it is his) Letters to the Thessalonians, the First Letter to the Corinthians, probably the Letter to the Philippians, and the Letter to the Galatians. He knows how to write well, and even today we recognize all the *pathos* with which his masterpieces are charged. And yet he affirms here, "You are the most beautiful letter I have written."

Then, continuing to elaborate on the metaphor, he adds, "written on [our] hearts."[1] Why doesn't he say "on *your* hearts"? (Some ancient manuscripts say "your" hearts, but it seems that "our" was the original reading.) Paul's mind is racing ahead: he is already thinking of the new covenant that is "written on our hearts," which applies to all the people of God.

The next affirmation—"known and read by all men"—is quite beautiful. Even though the letter is in hearts, it is legible; even though it is an inner reality, it is still visible. Paul is aware of the fact that communities radiate the joy of the gospel they receive, and he expressed this earlier in 1 Thessalonians 8-9:

For not only has the word of the Lord sounded forth from you in Macedonia and Achaia, but your faith in God has gone forth everywhere, so that we need not say anything. For they themselves report concerning us what a welcome we had among you, and how you turned to God from idols, to serve a living and true God.

The communities that speak of the gospel with joy become the apostle's letter of recommendation.

Paul uses the metaphor once more at the end: "You are a letter from Christ delivered by us." The preceding lesson about their being Paul's letter of recommendation is now superseded: it is in fact Christ himself who has written it and sent it. We see here a surprising christological development in the use of this image. Paul knows very well that Christ did not write it, but he knows that Christ can write on hearts and is saying, "The real author of you, my letter, is Christ; I was only his instrument." He keeps only a small role for himself: the letter is "delivered by us." It is a very beautiful expression in the Greek: *diakonetheisa*, I was the servant, the letter-carrier. He had his own experience in mind of dictating a letter to a secretary, as we see at the end of Romans 16:22: "I Tertius, the writer of this letter, greet you in the Lord."

The final affirmation: the letter is "written not with ink but with the Spirit of the living God, not on tablets of stone but on tablets of human hearts." It is the very Spirit of God who carves this letter in hearts. The perspective now expands to include Sinai and its summit. Paul moves from insight to insight through biblical allusions: "I will give you the tables of stone" (Exodus 24:12); the Lord gave Moses "the two tables of the testimony, tables of stone, written with the finger of God" (Exodus 31:18). "The

LORD said to Moses, 'Cut two tables of stone like the first; and I will write upon the tables the words that were on the first tables, which you broke'" (Exodus 34:1). The first covenant has been superseded: the new covenant is written not on tablets of stone, but "on tablets of human hearts."

We are reminded of Ezekiel 11:19: "I will give them one [a new] heart, and put a new spirit within them; I will take the stony heart out of their flesh and give them a heart of flesh."

We are reminded of Jeremiah 31:33: "This is the covenant which I will make with the house of Israel after those days, says the LORD: I will put my law within them, and I will write it upon their hearts."

Starting from an objection that had been made against him, and moving through a rapid succession of images, Paul arrives at Sinai and then at the new covenant prophesied by Ezekiel and Jeremiah, the covenant that Jesus writes on the heart of every believer.

Paul's Message for Us

What strikes us in what we have just heard? What message does it offer us?

What strikes me is *Paul's passion for his community*. Let us remember that we are dealing with an ungrateful, insolent community that has rebuffed him. It is a community that is hardly gratifying and has accused him of acting irresponsibly and insincerely. They have saddened him and made him suffer. The first two chapters of the letter report the accusations that have affected him and speak of his not wishing to return to Corinth in order to avoid further strife. We are seeing a community, then, that does not deserve much, but Paul, despite having received so many disappointments, remains passionate: "You are the best letter I have written; you are the work of the Spirit; you are the letter written by Christ."

His passion for the community also appears in 1 Corinthians 4:14-15:

> I do not write this to make you ashamed, but to admonish you as my beloved children. For though you have countless guides in Christ, you do not have many fathers. For I became your father in Christ Jesus though the gospel.

What an extraordinary relationship of suffering fatherhood! His statement in Galatians 4:19 is perhaps even stronger: "My little children, with whom I am again in travail until Christ be formed in you!" To "travail" is a maternal image. He is not only the father but also the mother of the community.

It seems clear that *Paul's passion and affection find a way into their hearts and, in the long run, are reciprocated.* His love goes further and is stronger than any resistance or disappointment. It gives life to the genuine family relationship that is established among those who do the will of God and listen to the word of the Lord. It is a relationship expressed so well and so tenderly in Philippians 1:7-8:

> It is right for me to feel thus about you all, because I hold you in my heart, for you are all partakers with me of grace, both in my imprisonment and in the defense and confirmation of the gospel. For God is my witness, how I yearn for you all with the affection of Christ Jesus.

Paul's affection, his love, is so stupendous that at a certain point, it is finally understood, accepted, and reciprocated.

There are many testimonies of the same kind today. I would like to quote from one of the many letters that people write me. This is from a person I have not met. After telling me which parish he belonged to, he shared this:

> The goal of this letter is to enable you to share in the joy that I and all the people in our parish experience every time we gather in church. We have a parish priest who is attentive to everyone, quick to smile and speak, with a greeting for everyone. His homilies touch our hearts, and I will not hide from you the fact that at times I begin to weep when I realize how much grace we have received. Yes, God has been so generous to us. Every idea we present to our priest is always well received by him, and he has committed himself to having everyone, even those who are farthest away, draw near to the Lord.

The climax of his praise comes in his comment about the associate pastor: "The associate pastor maintains such unity and collaboration of true brotherhood that as we observe it, we understand the commandment of love."

Perhaps this person wrote me in a moment of enthusiasm, but he certainly expresses a mutual affection. I have not ascertained who the parish priest is, preferring to think that things are always this way. It does mean, however, that relationships of affection exist, and people feel it deeply.

I experienced it myself and can share an example. In my pastoral letter, *La Madonna del Sabato santo*,[2] I asked the clergy and the faithful to help me take stock of their pastoral experience over the past few years, and I never imagined that I would receive so many responses. All the letters show that the people are full of gratitude, affection, and care. They show that pastoral love, despite appearances, is being reciprocated and brings joy.

There is still, in my opinion, a question that emerges from these three verses that I have commented on: Why is Paul proud of and pleased with his community in spite of the enormous defects and serious problems he has thoroughly criticized in both the First and Second Letters to the Corinthians?

He is proud and pleased, not only because his love is returned in the end, but for a further reason. He has invested a lot of himself in this community, by the grace of the Lord. He feels that the Lord himself has been involved and therefore perceives that his suffering is the suffering of Jesus. The community is dear to him to the extent that he has suffered for it and not so much because of the consolations he receives from it.

It is true of us as well that when we invest a lot in people, situations, and families that make us suffer, we love them more. If we are committed perhaps only superficially out of duty, we are not too concerned about their response. If, on the other hand, we have acted out of love, we suffer whenever there is not a response. But, through prayer and meditation, we become aware that it is not we, but rather the crucified Jesus, who has loved and invested a lot in these situations.

We can ask ourselves, "How passionately do I love my community and the people in it?"

We all know what joy we experience when a person or a group seeks God wholeheartedly or genuinely begins to follow a Christian path. Then it seems that our sacrifices have been repaid. However, even when this is not the immediate result, if we continue to put forth the effort to give of ourselves, we can rejoice that Christ is increasing in them while we are decreasing.

As a boy, I sometimes asked myself, "Do I love the Church?" It was not easy to answer, because I was taught that the priority clearly was love for Jesus.

I believe that experience shows that we begin to love the Church when we pray for her, when we invest much of our lives and our time in the Church. Then we discover that nothing concerning the Church leaves us indifferent, because we have cast our lot with her and have even identified ourselves with her.

1. Cardinal Martini uses "our" in this biblical text; the RSV uses "your" and gives "our" as an alternate word.

2. *La Madonna del Sabato santo* ["Our Lady of Holy Saturday"], pastoral letter for 2000–2001, August 6, 2000.

CHAPTER 6

Suffering and Consolation

Paul's Second Letter to the Corinthians is a text I have reflected on for many years, and I cherish it because it shows us Paul in the midst of his ministry. The apostle is not full of illusions and does not delude himself like we sometimes do. In this text, Paul appears, we could say, in the tough nitty-gritty of his apostolate. After more than twenty years of ministry with many trials because of disappointments and difficulties, he speaks as a servant of the gospel in the midst of daily struggles. For that reason we experience him as very similar to us.

Paul's Three Trials

While he is writing this letter, Paul is basically experiencing *three main trials*.

The *first* is feeling rejected by the majority of his Jewish brethren. He thought that Jesus' primary intention was to entrust him with the mission of preaching to his brothers and sisters, as he had done when he went from city to city visiting the synagogues. He had deluded himself into thinking that, in spite of the unavoidable difficulties, the Jews would have understood. However, the illusion faded, and the mission failed. In the Letter to the Romans, dated around this time, we see that the apostle still has some hope, but he has resigned himself to the fact that a rift has occurred, and he suffers enormously because of it. In the Corinthians text it is easy to see that this was one of the first great disappointments of his ministry: those to whom the word was primarily addressed did not respond. Added to Paul's sufferings are questions: Why did God permit this? Why are things going this way? Why was the word not received by those to whom it was directly and primarily addressed?

This trial recalls for me the pain that Cardinal Giovanni Battista Montini [who later became Pope Paul VI] expressed about the distance kept by the working class, the rift, he would say, between the Church and the world of simple, humble people— especially the workers—who should have been the first addressees of the gospel.

Paul's *second* trial comes from the internal conflicts within the community. The apostle dreamed of united, brotherly communities, full of enthusiasm and unanimity. Instead, his disappointing experience—already expressed in his First Letter to the Corinthians but reaching its culmination here—is of a community in which there are many serious divisions. The divisions are not only internal but also surround him—misunderstandings and various kinds of mistrust about him. Thus, the Second Letter to the Corinthians is written precisely to clarify the misunderstandings, the mistrust, and the prejudices emerging from his encounters with this community.

The *third* trial consists of inner struggles, which Paul mentions discretely but occasionally in an open way. It is difficult to know exactly what these sufferings were. Bearing in mind Paul's temperament, we could imagine his highs and lows, i.e., periods of enthusiasm that would alternate with periods of depression, fatigue, frustrations in his ministry, and exhausting work.

Because of the three trials the apostle is undergoing, we experience the Second Letter to the Corinthians as very relevant to us. It is useful for us to reflect on it when any of us, in our own way, experiences various trials; it is important to find the right attitude to handle them. To say that Paul is in the midst of his ministry means not only that he is in the middle of his apostolic activity but also that he is in the middle of his suffering.

Impressions from the Second Letter to the Corinthians

In reflecting again on the letter as a whole, I am left with three specific impressions.

Above all I am struck by the *very strong confidence Paul has in his charism*, which he expresses in every possible way.

In contrast to the difficult situations we have already mentioned, what emerges is the picture of a man who is absolutely convinced that everything around him could fail but not his charism. Even when he describes his sufferings in the starkest manner, what clearly emerges is his absolute certainty regarding the charism that has been given to him regarding his vocation and regarding his mission, understood as a gift of the Holy Spirit. He judges everything else in the light of this gift of the Spirit, and during trials his charism becomes even stronger and more authentic.

This is very impressive and wonderful; there is something divine here, because the onslaught of trials against him could have actually led to a diminishment of his confidence or to timidity. His trials could have made him ask the following questions: "Is this really my charism? Is it that strong? Should I completely trust it?"

Paul's confidence in his charism, as he expresses it, gives us strength too. I can say that I have been brought back to clarity about my charism as a priest and bishop many times through the words in this letter.

Everything else can fade away, but not the certainty about his charism, as he writes in the Letter to the Romans: "Who shall separate us from the love of Christ?" (8:35). Internal and external adversities may occur, and many things may fail; nevertheless, nothing will be able to separate us from the love of God that is in Christ Jesus our Lord, who has chosen me and called me.

This very strong confidence in his charism is lived out in *humble, obscure, and very painful circumstances*. Even though there are individual situations that comfort the apostle, the totality of his circumstances is, nevertheless, humble. We are dealing with an apostolate that reaches, in fact, few people. Paul was hoping to reach a huge group (at least the Jewish people), and instead he reaches small communities that have no influence on public opinion. And these humble, obscure, and painful circumstances give rise to many trials: people's pettiness and inconstancy, betrayal by friends, the subterfuges Paul sees himself surrounded by, and the exhausting task of discerning between true and false apostles and a mishmash of doctrines and propositions.

Circumstances like these, which would normally have caused confusion, sadness, and a sense of loss, are in sharp contrast to his very strong confidence in his charism. Everything else may crumble, but not this certainty.

Finally, what stands out in several pages of his letter is that Paul *was living through all of this with an unconditional, unshakable love for his community*. We see that people who are somewhat mean and hostile to Paul are continually the objects of his most tender, constructive love. The community tries to marginalize him, to taint him with insincerity, but he fights to present himself as a loving father, not at all angered or embittered about anything. Starting from this vantage point, he presents himself to the community with authority and emotional intensity.

There is something extraordinary about Paul's love if we think of how easily we retreat into ourselves when we are not well received or when some people's welcome is not enough to counterbalance the cold, critical, reserved, and distant welcome by others.

We see Paul's profound suffering in this letter, but we do not find one single statement that could be interpreted as his retreating into himself.

This letter is real medicine for any Christian who is experiencing trials. It is like nourishment that reinvigorates because of its powerful words. For the person who believes they come from the Holy Spirit, these words are so relevant that they can restore our self-confidence by preserving a larger vision for us in the midst of our minor, petty circumstances, and they demonstrate a love that never ceases to correct but is steadfast.

A Reading from 2 Corinthians 1:1-11:

¹Paul, an apostle of Christ Jesus by the will of God, and Timothy our brother.

To the church of God which is at Corinth, with all the saints who are in the whole of Achaia:

²Grace to you and peace from God our Father and the Lord Jesus Christ.

³Blessed be the God and Father of our Lord Jesus Christ, the Father of mercies and God of all comfort, ⁴who comforts us in all our affliction, so that we may be able to comfort those who are in any affliction, with the comfort with which we ourselves are comforted by God. ⁵For as we share abundantly in Christ's sufferings, so through Christ we share abundantly in comfort too. ⁶If we are afflicted, it is for your comfort and salvation; and if we are comforted, it is for your comfort, which you experience when you patiently endure the same sufferings that we suffer. ⁷Our hope for you is

unshaken; for we know that as you share in our sufferings, you will also share in our comfort.

[8]For we do not want you to be ignorant, brethren, of the affliction we experienced in Asia; for we were so utterly, unbearably crushed that we despaired of life itself. [9]Why, we felt that we had received the sentence of death; but that was to make us rely not on ourselves but on God who raises the dead; [10]he delivered us from so deadly a peril, and he will deliver us; on him we have set our hope that he will deliver us again. [11]You also must help us by prayer, so that many will give thanks on our behalf for the blessing granted us in answer to many prayers.

Consolation for Suffering

What title could we give this passage as a whole? The edition of the Bible that I am looking at has an excellent title for it: *Suffering and Consolation*. It is a title that speaks for itself because it does not say "suffering and joy," which is the usual experience we have in life. In life we experience suffering and joy, seeking a balance between the two, since joy all the time would be hard to imagine, and suffering all the time would be unbearable.

Paul's attitude is quite different. He is not trying to find a balance between suffering and joy, but to experience the sufferings and the consolations that are in—and that come from—the sufferings. In my opinion, this is a remarkable insight. He does not see suffering and joy as elements of a person's journey; instead, he sees that suffering and consolation come from the very afflictions he is enduring.

We see it clearly in the text: the God and Father of our Lord

Jesus Christ comforts us in all our afflictions (see verses 3-4). This does not refer to a generic kind of joy but rather to a consolation that is *within* the affliction he is facing. The following verse helps us to penetrate more fully the tribulation-consolation relationship: "We share abundantly in Christ's sufferings" (verse 5). These are no longer Paul's sufferings but those of Christ, and we understand that the apostle instinctively lives out those sufferings, not as his unique personal destiny, but as the sufferings of Christ in him. They belong to the ministry that the Lord Jesus entrusted to him and therefore to the shared life that he lives in Christ. He calls them "Christ's sufferings" since they come to him precisely because he has committed himself to ministry out of love for the Lord.

To the extent that these kinds of sufferings abound—they are numerous and frequent, not few and far between—there is corresponding comfort: "Through Christ we share abundantly in comfort too" (verse 5). There is a very tight-knit relationship between the suffering of Jesus in him and the consolation from Jesus in him. We can say that Paul interprets his experience of personal and community trials as part of the mystery of death-resurrection. As he enters into the mystery of death, the mystery of Jesus' resurrection abounds in him as well, and he experiences it as comfort, as consolation.

Entering into Trials

Moving on to the *meditatio* of verses 3-5, we wonder what connection exists between suffering and consolation that can cause consolation to arise in and from the suffering.

The connection is that consolation results from entering into trials. The consolation is not located alongside or next to the trials, like a reward distinct from the trial; rather, it results from entering into the trials.

We can enter into trials physically or even psychologically, but when we do not enter them existentially, then the core of our being is not involved in the trial. In so doing, we close ourselves off to the consolation of Jesus. Not having entered into a trial with our whole being, we do not then experience the consolation inside the trial.

This phenomenon is very interesting. I have experienced it myself, and I will try to explain what I mean. Trials can be of different sorts: physical or emotional weariness, moodiness, weariness from daily serving, feelings of repugnance, feelings of aversion to people, situations, or events. They involve us physically and psychologically, but we do not enter them existentially because we do not look them in the face. We deny them; we marginalize them; we lay them aside, perhaps out of fear of not being able to face them head on. In so doing, we consider them as phenomena alongside our existence. We believe that they should not exist, so it is better to absorb them unconsciously. We practice a kind of psychological anesthesia toward such trials.

I believe that sometimes we deprive ourselves of the strength we could derive from entering into the sufferings of Christ precisely because when facing them, we hold our breath, we close our eyes, and we keep moving forward the same way as always, without dealing with them specifically in prayer and in conversation with Christ. Going about it this way, we do not internalize them, and the trials remain like foreign bodies: they are not integrated into our lives, and thus they cannot be transformed into consolation.

Having attended many parish pastoral councils, for example, I am aware that people can encounter quite a few of these trials, frustrations, perhaps minor internal divisions, difficulties in their relationship with the pastor, and especially weariness and dissatisfaction in their isolation with respect to the larger parish. (The community does not know us, does not appreciate us, does not value our work, etc.) These kinds of things would seem to call for a missionary spirit. On the contrary, however, it seems to me that people endure these trials with a certain instinctive and unconscious resentment, bad humor, and almost irritation toward themselves and others. They do not go through them as the trials of Christ, as sufferings that Christ and the Christian encounter, embracing them and then experiencing in them the power of Christ. When they are embraced, however, we can speak much more freely about them, with honesty and courage, almost without self-concern and with that spirit of gospel passion and fire that is precisely characteristic of all of Paul's discourse in the Second Letter to the Corinthians.

The apostle does not blame himself, he does not have regrets, and he does not let himself be stopped, as do many communities that are indeed good and generous and desire to devote themselves to real service to Christ. They still have not understood what the apostles themselves endured many hardships to learn: only by entering into the trial and into the cross of Christ are we able to share in his consolation.

These communities seem to have Peter's attitude when he says to Jesus, "God forbid, Lord! This shall never happen to you" (Matthew 16:22). It is an attitude that exclaims, "How could this ever happen? Things should not be this way!" They have not moved on to the second stage in the Gospel of Mark (see Mark 8:35), i.e., the acceptance of Christ's trials in order to be consoled in them with the power of his consolation, with the grace of the Spirit's consolation, which only gets poured out through the acceptance of such trials.

From the beginning through the end of the letter, we find remarkable instructions for our daily lives and for the life of our communities. Verses 4 and 5 offer us an initial reflection: consolation derives *from the sufferings* of Christ in us. It is very meaningful to speak of the sufferings of Christ in us. It sheds a different light on things when I understand that it is not just a question of my weaknesses, my lack of success, or my personal defeats but rather of the sufferings of Christ in me. Then I understand that suffering is a way that Christ is at work in me and that it is he who suffers because of my weakness, which is caused and affected by the difficult circumstances of my Christian life.

Apostolic Consolation

Verses 6 and 7 in this chapter of 2 Corinthians emphasize that this consolation *is for others*.

This very important apostolic consolation, the work of the Holy Spirit in the believing servant of the gospel, is not for himself; it is not like the joys of life that we can think are given to compensate us for our trials. Apostolic consolation is directed toward others. "If we are afflicted, it is for your comfort and salvation; and if we are comforted, it is for your comfort" (verse 6).

Paul sees these trials and the subsequent consolations as an integral aspect of his service. His entering into trials is for others; it is not merely incidental but is rather a basic component of his ministry. This is what I tried to say in other ways in my pastoral letter *Itinerari educativi*[1] when I spoke about the failures in catechetical formation. The failures are not simply incidental to the formation, but rather a basic component, in that through these failures I can arrive at an effective and formative love of God.

Consolations, therefore, are for others. In verse 7, I see something that I have confronted to my own embarrassment: "Our hope for you is unshaken; for we know that as you share in our sufferings, you will also share in our comfort."

I think about certain meetings that sometimes irritate me because of the pettiness, the lack of breathing space or open-mindedness of the people who are all wrapped up in themselves. Meetings with some of these pastoral councils can make one's heart ache, because the people do not succeed in seeing the signs of the gospel, or they see very few of them. I am overcome by a sense of struggle, almost of frustration: How hard this is! What can be done?

Facing my temptation with the words of Paul, I realize I would not be able to instinctively say, "Our hope for you is unshaken; for we know that as you share in our sufferings, you will also share in our comfort." A person needs a strong vision of faith to see the struggles and the defects of the community—obstacles, divisions, prejudices—as suffering that overcomes them. I ask myself, if a group of young people came to me about their struggles, their lack of unity, their failures, would I succeed in saying, "In every case, my hope for you is unshaken, since I am convinced that sharing in the suffering, you will indeed share in the comfort"?

The challenge is helping a community or a group of young people to take on this kind of approach so that it could become true about them.

The Life-Threatening Trial

"The Life-Threatening Trial" could be the subtitle for verses 8 and 9: "For we do not want you to be ignorant, brethren, of the affliction we experienced in Asia; for we were so utterly, unbearably crushed that we despaired of life itself" (verse 8).

Paul gives us a glimpse at some diminishment of his strength, which in other parts of the letter appears so scintillating and forceful.

I said earlier that Paul expresses a high degree of confidence in his charism in this letter, yet here he confesses that the trial he and Timothy experienced in Asia—probably caused by external persecution, sadness, very deep disappointment about the community, perhaps times of lower mental energy—left them "so utterly, unbearably crushed."

Sometimes we, too, can feel ourselves unbearably crushed beyond our strength. However, when we take accurate stock of the situation, we realize that things could be worse and that the Lord has spared us again.

But even if we should get to the place where we need to say that we are "so utterly, unbearably crushed," then we would be like the apostle who "despaired of life itself," meaning that we feel that nothing works, that everything is over. However, Paul goes on to say, "We felt that we had received the sentence of death; but that was to make us rely not on ourselves but on God who raises the dead" (verse 9). We see that the paschal mystery is not an abstraction for Paul. It is the God who raises the dead who also rescues me from a dead-end situation that has no escape or possible solution.

Authentic Relationships

Verses 10 and 11 have the *involvement or participation of the community* as their theme. Paul is saying, "If I have overcome this trial that, I must admit, was very, very difficult, it is thanks to you and your prayers. Continue to pray for me, and thank God on my behalf."

I ask myself, "Have I ever had this kind of relationship of trust with a community?" Have I ever said, "Pray for me because I find myself in a difficult situation," or "I found myself in a very difficult situation, and I have come through it thanks to your prayers and to your standing with me"?

Reading Paul's words, we are amazed at the freedom of his sharing with the community: "He delivered us from so deadly a peril, and he will deliver us; on him we have set our hope that he will deliver us again" (verse 10).

You may perhaps have noticed that participation is easier when the issue of death or suffering arises due to physical suffering. In that case, when a person shares about it, the community's involvement happens immediately. There are, in fact, communities that immediately reconcile with their pastor if there is a case of a serious or terminal illness. A transformation of the people occurs, and the human dimension of the relationships becomes clear.

I recall with emotion an example of the serious physical suffering of Monsignor Filippo Franceschi, the bishop of Padua. Once the diocesan community was aware of his health problem and he had asked to receive a public anointing of the sick by the priests during the celebration of Holy Thursday, a remarkable solidarity and unity developed. The people profoundly understood the situation of their frail pastor, threatened by sickness and tested by terrible sufferings. They felt themselves partly responsible and called to a serious consideration of a more human and genuine relationship with their bishop; they stopped criticizing him and demanding things from him.

Things like this happen often. Obviously, we should not desire such suffering to occur, but this situation is a symbol of a more authentic relationship that Paul teaches us about and that we should now reflect upon in silence before God. We should ask, "Lord, how do I live through the trials Paul lived through? Do I succeed in speaking like he does? Are his sentiments mine? How far am I from having those sentiments?"

Lord, give me the consolation of the Spirit!

1. Cardinal Carlo M. Martini, *Itinerari educativi* ["Journeys in Formation"], pastoral letter for 1988–89, July 31, 1988.

CHAPTER 7

The Mystery of Iniquity

A Reading from 2 Thessalonians 2:1-12

[1]Now concerning the coming of our Lord Jesus Christ and our assembling to meet him, we beg you, brethren, [2]not to be quickly shaken in mind or excited, either by spirit or by word, or by letter purporting to be from us, to the effect that the day of the Lord has come. [3]Let no one deceive you in any way; for that day will not come, unless the rebellion comes first, and the man of lawlessness is revealed, the son of perdition, [4]who opposes and exalts himself against every so-called god or object of worship, so that he takes his seat in the temple of God, proclaiming himself to be God. [5]Do you not remember that when I was still with you I told you this? [6]And you know what is restraining him now so that he may be revealed in his time. [7]For the mystery of lawlessness [iniquity] is already at work; only he who now restrains it will do so until he is out of the way. [8]And then the lawless one will be revealed, and the Lord Jesus will slay him with the breath of his mouth and destroy him by his appearing and his coming. [9]The coming of the lawless one by the activity of Satan will be with all power and with pretended signs and wonders, [10]and with all wicked deception for those who are to perish, because they refused to love the truth and so be saved. [11]Therefore God sends upon them a strong delusion, to make them believe what is false, [12]so that all may be condemned who did not believe the truth but had pleasure in unrighteousness.

The broad context of our passage is the entire Second Letter to the Thessalonians. Like the First Letter to the Thessalonians, it is entirely focused on eschatological themes.

Paul on the *Parousia*

Paul's Second Letter to the Thessalonians gets to the heart of the matter and deals with the main topic of the *parousia* and the issues related to it.

Above all, *Paul clears the field of inappropriate ideas,* if not errors, that have insinuated themselves into the community, causing doubt and confusion about the imminence of the day of the Lord (verses 1-3a). We could call the Thessalonians Jehovah Witnesses *ante litteram* (before that term was first used). They were a kind of sect that arose because of anxiety about the imminent coming of the Lord. The apostle admonishes them to not panic.

Having cleared the field, *he lays out his thought* about the *parousia* in a very original interplay of light and dark: "For that day [of the Lord] will not come, unless the rebellion comes first, and the man of iniquity[2] is revealed, the son of perdition" (verse 3b). From the religious point of view, "rebellion" or "apostasy" indicates a turning away from God or, more precisely, abandoning him in favor of other deities. The phrase "the man of lawlessness" symbolizes all the worldly powers that, rather than serving humanity, become wicked mechanisms of exploitation; the term encompasses all the idolatry and the ideologies that mythologize human power.

A gloomy summary of the "son of perdition" follows in verse 4 but is interrupted in verse 5: "Do you not remember that when I was still with you I told you this?" Paul then takes up his discourse again: "You know what is restraining him now so that he may be revealed in his time" (verse 6). No Scripture scholar has been able to explain exactly what *katechon* (what is restraining him) means. In any case, the apostle alludes to the fact that the worst has not yet happened. Nevertheless, even though the worst has not yet happened, verse 7 tells us that "the mystery of iniquity is *already at work*," *energeitai*; it is active and energized; "only he who now restrains it will do so until he is out of the way."

At that time, iniquity will reveal itself in all its strength but at the same time, Christ will be revealed as the real conqueror because he is able to annihilate evil. The final and definitive condemnation of all the workers of iniquity is an original and rather vivid way of assuring the Thessalonians of the superiority of the good (see verses 8b-12). Therefore, in order to understand the *parousia,* we need to shed light on the mystery of iniquity that operates presumptuously, assuming divine prerogatives for itself. It is already operating in power, but it has not yet reached the height of its wicked manifestation that will explode at the end of history. Christ the Lord, however, will win the victory.

I could summarize the text with a statement from Jacques Maritain that offers an interpretation for humanity's path through history: "The advance of history is a twofold simultaneous progress in good and evil."[1] There is, in fact, something true about this insight, because it is rather difficult to find in the centuries preceding ours a force as evil, for example, as the one that was manifested at Auschwitz. The power of evil on earth, therefore, is growing, but at the same time the power of the Lord Jesus is also growing, and Jesus will one day destroy the mystery of evil with the breath of his mouth.

We belong to that period of history Paul refers to when he says "the mystery of iniquity is already at work," even though it is not fully manifested.

There are two ways of understanding the phrase "the mystery of iniquity."

The first way—which I do not find persuasive—interprets the word "mystery" in the positive sense of a divine plan and affirms that in the divine plan of salvation, there is a place for iniquity. Iniquity would be the darkness in the *chiaroscuro*—the contrast between light and dark—of the divine plan in history.

The second way, which seems much more logical to me, interprets "the mystery of iniquity" in its more literal sense. The mystery of salvation (see Romans 16:25-26; Ephesians 3:8ff; Colossians 1:25ff) refers to the eternal plan that God unfolds in history for the salvation of humanity. The *mysterium* of the Scriptures has its full revelation in Christ and will be brightly revealed in the *parousia*. In a parallel way, but as a counterpoint, there is a *mysterium iniquitatis*, a "plan of perdition," a kind of development in history that, with its own logic and intelligence, plots the destruction of human beings, their humiliation, their oppression, and their annihilation.

It seems to me that this is what St. Paul means by the "mystery of iniquity" in 2 Thessalonians 2:7.

Meditatio on the Mystery of Iniquity

After rereading the passage that is one of the most difficult and controversial in the New Testament, I would like to examine the "mystery of iniquity" more systematically to understand at least something about what it is. Since iniquity is not something that can be grasped rationally, it is a mystery that cannot be put into words. It is possible, however, to observe it in its historical effects without our having to delve into the theological dimensions of evil, which are difficult to access because they involve an abyss that is revealed only to the believing conscience.

On the phenomenological level, we see a triple mystery of evil: evil in relation to individuals, to nations, and to ideologies.

The evil related to *individuals* includes all forms of deviation from the good or of the absence of good that harm human beings and that we experience every day. I am thinking of sicknesses, of physical and psychological suffering, of premature deaths, of pain, of malice. Then, there is a list of crimes committed by individuals: fraud, theft, assault, rape, prostitution, drug dealing, murder, corruption, and injustice—a vast range of offenses dealt with by the justice system. The numbers furnished every year by the state prosecutors—conservative numbers—are very high and indicate only the crimes that are reported! However, these numbers are always smaller than the number of acts of goodness. All this ferment of evil committed by individuals pervades humanity, but it is simply the first aspect of the mystery of iniquity.

Beyond individual evil, there is *collective* evil, the evil that can come from nations, organizations, or ethnic groups. It occurs when moral disorders become public and infectious, and as a result, individuals need to perform heroic acts to extricate themselves from the pressure of collective sin and the structures of injustice. This is what happened in the concentration camps, where everyone was obliged to do evil and where even the prisoners themselves were grouped in hierarchies among themselves in such a way that some were forced to perform evil acts against others.

"Accomplices" to collective or structural evil include the acquiescence of good people, mass laziness, the refusal to think, the eagerness for entertainment and success, and the need for immediate gratification. These attitudes enable evil to advance and allow people to avoid pronouncing judgment on the situation as a whole. On the opposite side, another "accomplice" includes a fanatical enthusiasm that dulls people's sensitivity to moral evils and to the suffering of others. For this reason, historians are still puzzled today by the acquiescence of the German people to such very grave crimes.

The clearest example of concentrated collective evil is the concentration camp. We see other examples of widespread corruption: a recent bribery scandal, which is essentially a conglomeration of evils, and many people got involved almost against their will; uncontrolled rioting where one disorder leads quickly to another; and bloody tribal and ethnic conflicts.

Human history would not be so wicked if evil deeds were done only by individuals, because crimes, even when they are numerous, do not succeed in destroying a society. A society falls when the evil is collective and infects whole groups, pitting them against one another.

In that regard, we need to be vigilant and attentive. We need to develop an *examination of cultural conscience*, recognizing that it is an uphill process as we try to understand the complicities, omissions, and wrongs that are involved. Otherwise, collective evil spreads and destroys humanity.

However, this is still not the end of the phenomenological analysis of the mystery of iniquity.

There is a third kind of evil that heightens the first and second kinds, and it is the evil of *intellectual aberrations or ideologies* in which iniquity is lifted up as a principle or ideal for life and action.

Iniquity reaches this level when moral deviations become legitimized or directly rationalized through ideologies or philosophies. It is then that evil takes root and asserts its power. As Paul affirms, iniquity does not simply set itself up as an object of religious worship in the temple of God, but it also sets itself up as an object of worship in the temple of science or philosophy.

Isaiah referred to this situation:

Woe to those who call evil good and good evil,
who put darkness for light
and light for darkess. (Isaiah 5:20)

Here we are facing the greatest evil that encompasses all other evils and that transforms all of them into a flood of disorder in history. And it is precisely the rationalized legitimization of evil that is at the heart of the mystery of evil, the historical triumph of Satan, the wicked deception we read about in 2 Thessalonians 2:10-11: those who "believe what is false" will "perish." Above and beyond simply doing evil through weakness or passion, they believe what is false.

Only this can explain the major moral aberrations, the legalized massacres, the ferocity of ethnic cleansing. Only this can explain something like Auschwitz, which is the fruit of a demonic theory of evil being portrayed as good.

It would be interesting to reread, in this regard, parts of Giuseppe Dossetti's preface for the book *Le querce di Monte Sole*,[3] which he wrote after having spent two days in Auschwitz meditating and reflecting on the mystery of iniquity. Dossetti dedicated the book to the 250 people killed at Monte Sole—elderly people, women, and children—and he wonders how a system of such perverse and gratuitous destruction could arise. He attributes it to an evil that presents itself as an idea or an interpretation of history or that presents itself as philosophy and culture. When violence and injustice are legalized and legitimized by a dominant class, evil multiplies without resistance—apart from the resistance of a few heroes—and that society falls into a darkened condition. According to the apostle's words, we are not so very far away from that, even if iniquity has not yet been totally unleashed.

Instinctively, we tell ourselves that the worst will not happen, that we will commit all our energy to prevent iniquity from spreading everywhere, but this mystery is strongly at work (*energeitai*). Woe, then, to those who lower their guard, deluding themselves that there will not be another Auschwitz! Human wickedness continually lies in ambush; the mystery of evil's shrewdness does not cease; the "son of perdition," the "man of iniquity," still needs to be revealed in his fullness.

This is a blind spot we are afraid to think about, but recent history highlights our error in not thinking about it and prods us to correct that.

Our Attitude toward the Mystery of Evil

I know that I am speaking haltingly on this topic, so I will briefly suggest some points that will perhaps help each of you to personally reflect and apply what we have been considering.

1. *Do not be surprised*, or do not cry out about what a catastrophe it is, if signs of the mystery of iniquity begin to appear, as though it were an unexpected event that should not be occurring. It is true that evil should not occur, but Jesus and the authors of the New Testament admonished us at length about raging against the mystery of evil, whether in its large-scale form or—often more crucifying—in its more commonplace form in daily life. History is marked by evil probably destined to increase, not to decrease, and so it is out of place for us, whenever we face an instance of iniquity, to ask, "Why didn't the kingdom of God triumph over

it?" We know that from the very beginning when the kingdom appeared, it sprang up in a field of evil, in a world darkened by the power of the evil one. For this reason, alternate interpretations of history that do not take this into account are ingenuous, insufficient, and delusional.

May the Lord give us the clarity fitting for people who are aware of being called to face the mystery of iniquity in history.

2. *Maintain a vigilant attitude in order to discover the unfolding of the plan of salvation in the heart of the mystery of evil.* We need to be aware, on one hand, of the current shape of iniquity, which is always ongoing, and, on the other hand, of the flowering of the mystery of salvation in a field full of weeds where the good wheat is also growing. Only this kind of twofold orientation avoids bitterness, frustration, and pessimism.

We are encouraged to reach this maturity, to become capable of a cultural analysis that tries to understand the components— even when they seem anonymous and insignificant—of the plan of God and of the plots of Satan, of the mystery of salvation and of the mystery of evil. We are invited to be vigilant prophets.

3. *Expect to be hurt and wounded in some way by the mystery of evil.* Remember the words of my episcopal motto: *pro veritate adversa diligere* (to love adversity for the sake of truth).[4] We should expect to be touched by adversity, to be pierced, trusting that the Lord will preserve us from being crushed.

Everything that I have said about the mystery of individual evil, collective evil, and ideological evil is still little or nothing with respect to the theological mystery, that is, evil as rebellion against God and as a rejection of God and of his merciful love.

This is an abyss that we cannot fully understand except in some small measure, when we contemplate the crucified One, when we linger before the torn and wounded heart of Jesus.

We beseech you, Heart of Christ, pierced by human evil, help us understand at least a little of what you experienced in the Garden of Gethsemane regarding the mystery of iniquity. Help us see it as you understood it, in such a way that we can succeed, in union with you, in combating and overcoming it in our flesh and in our lives.

1. Jacques Maritain, *On the Philosophy of History*, ed. Joseph W. Evans (London: Geoffrey Bles, 1959), p. 8.

2. The Italian text that Cardinal Martini uses is translated as "iniquity," although the RSV uses the term "lawlessness."

3. Luciano Gherardi, *Le querce di Monte Sole* [The Oaks of Monte Sole] (Bologna: Il Mulino, 1986). The book details the background and the story of the German massacre of Italian men, women, and children in Monte Sole in the autumn of 1944.

4. The Latin phrase is taken from Gregory the Great's *Ars pastoralis* [*Pastoral Rule*], 1, 3.

CHAPTER 8

The Word of the Cross

I firmly believe that the mystery of the cross is the key to the history of salvation, and I have spoken about that on many occasions. I recall, for example, the section from *Regola di vita del cristiano ambrosiano* where I say, under the subheading "The 'Suffering' God and the Law of the Cross,"

> How I want everyone to . . . understand that the mystery of a crucified and risen God is the key to human existence and the essence of the gospel and of our faith! Yet the waves of our resistance smash up against the rock of this "paschal mystery." Nevertheless, it is precisely in the paschal mystery that the connections between death and life, sorrow and joy, failure and success, frustration and desire, humiliation and exaltation, despair and hope, are reestablished. When the "law of the cross" touches us, it unsettles us, and we are profoundly disturbed. But only through the law of the cross does complete freedom from evil occur, as we accept its consequences for us to forgive the evil and to overcome it as Jesus did on the cross.[1]

I want to reflect with you in a very simple way. After an initial look at Philippians 3:18 (which deals with the enemies of the cross), we will then devote ourselves to the *lectio* and *meditatio* of 1 Corinthians 1–2.

For many, of whom I have often told you and now tell you even with tears, live as enemies of the cross of Christ. (Philippians 3:18)

This verse makes us pause, because St. Paul is speaking about the Christian community when he affirms that many do not understand the mystery of the cross. The word translated "live" means "conduct oneself." The issue is an enmity against the cross that is manifested in the lifestyle and in the everyday circumstances of so many who call themselves Christians.

It is also striking that Paul has already denounced this error "often" (it weighs on his heart), and now "with tears" he repeats it. He weeps with great sorrow, as he does when he thinks of the fate of Israel, which he talks about beginning in Romans 9.

Who are the enemies of the cross of Christ? Instinctively we think of libertines and licentious people who have a hedonistic view of life. Actually, the text points instead to some sects, and Paul weeps when he sees that they are engaged in useless and harmful sacrifices. Practically speaking, the enemies are those Jewish Christians that we read about at the beginning of Philippians 3: "Look out for the dogs, look out for the evil-workers, look out for those who mutilate the flesh [i.e., those who require circumcision]" (verse 2). These people are convinced that they can save themselves through their own works, through their sacrifices and their renunciations, through circumcision and observance of the law, and they do not have faith in the cross of Jesus.

That Paul has these kinds of Christians in mind is confirmed in verse 19 where he describes them with three characteristics:

Their end is destruction, their god is the belly [they want to save themselves through the rules about clean and unclean foods], and they glory in their shame [the sign of circumcision in their bodies], with minds set on earthly things [tied to human observances].

Immediately after, he adds, as a contrast, "Our commonwealth is in heaven" (verse 20).

It is not easy, therefore, to identify the enemies of the cross of Christ according to our modern categories. One Scripture scholar described them as those who reject the cross as the key to interpreting Christian existence and embrace instead a focus on enthusiastic participation right now in the triumphant, victorious glory of the risen One.

Using more simplified language, perhaps we can distinguish three types of enemies of the cross:

The first type, the one St. Paul most directly targets in this text, consists in *those who seek justification through the works of the law,* rejecting the salvation that comes only from the forgiving love of God.

In addition, there are *those who close themselves off from facing a crucified God,* i.e., who reject the cross as the way God has chosen to redeem the world and as the perspective for life according to God's plan.

And then there are *those who reject the mystery of their own cross,* who do not want to make this ultimate association with the love of Jesus, in contrast to the way Paul lives: "Now I rejoice in my sufferings for your sake, and in my flesh I complete what is lacking in Christ's afflictions" (Colossians 1:24).

This third category is quite broad, but it could be articulated theologically, quite simply, as related to the absence of a spirit of sacrifice. It is above all a lack of faith in God, who loves us so much and forgives us so much.

I will address this in a detailed way by commenting on the passage for our *lectio divina*, 1 Corinthians 1:17–2:5, which the reading of Philippians 3:18 introduced.

A Reading from 1 Corinthians 1:17–2:5:

[17]For Christ did not send me to baptize but to preach the gospel, and not with eloquent wisdom, lest the cross of Christ be emptied of its power.

[18]For the word of the cross is folly to those who are perishing, but to us who are being saved it is the power of God. [19]For it is written,

"I will destroy the wisdom of the wise,

and the cleverness of the clever I will thwart."

[20]Where is the wise man? Where is the scribe? Where is the debater of this age? Has not God made foolish the wisdom of the world? [21]For since, in the wisdom of God, the world did not know God through wisdom, it pleased God through the folly of what we preach to save those who believe. [22]For Jews demand signs and Greeks seek wisdom, [23]but we preach Christ crucified, a stumbling block to Jews and folly to Gentiles, [24]but to those who are called, both Jews and Greeks, Christ the power of God and the wisdom of God. [25]For the foolishness of God is wiser than men, and the weakness of God is stronger than men.

[26]For consider your call, brethren; not many of you were wise according to worldly standards, not many were powerful, not many were of noble birth; [27]but God chose what is foolish in the world to shame the wise, God chose what is weak in the world to shame the strong, [28]God chose what is low and despised in the world, even things that

are not, to bring to nothing things that are, [29]so that no human being might boast in the presence of God. [30]He is the source of your life in Christ Jesus, whom God made our wisdom, our righteousness and sanctification and redemption; [31]therefore, as it is written, "Let him who boasts, boast of the Lord."

[2:1]When I came to you, brethren, I did not come proclaiming to you the testimony of God in lofty words or wisdom. [2]For I decided to know nothing among you except Jesus Christ and him crucified. And I was with you in weakness and in much fear and trembling; [4]and my speech and my message were not in plausible words of wisdom, but in demonstration of the Spirit and of power, [5]that your faith might not rest in the wisdom of men but in the power of God.

The Context (verse 17)

The context of this verse is the first letter that Paul writes to the Corinthians recalling his apostolate and recalling his preaching that had subsequently led to divisions among the believers. It is thus a kind of rereading by Paul, and it is important because it probably expresses a new beginning in his preaching. This also explains the richness of the passage. The apostle describes the substance of his preaching by using wordplay that contrasts the wisdom of the world and the word of the cross. The antithesis is already mentioned in verse 17, which is part of the preceding section: he did not evangelize "with eloquent wisdom, lest the cross of Christ be emptied of its power."

This kind of juxtaposition pervades the whole passage that I have chosen for this reflection, and it was written with great emotional intensity.

We note the contrast between the words "wisdom, power, cleverness" and the words "folly, stumbling block, weakness." While the first group of words characterizes a worldly approach, the second characterizes God's approach. Everything is played out through this set of contrasts, until Paul turns the application of the words upside down, and then the foolishness of God becomes the highest wisdom, and the weakness of God becomes the strongest display of power (verse 25). This reversal of meaning in the antithesis is very interesting.

Certainly, the passage is not without rhetoric, but it is a rhetoric that emerges from a sorrowful experience and from an astounding mystical insight. For that reason, it is a very valuable text.

Exposition of the Passage

In the first part, verse 18, we read the thesis statement for everything that follows: "The word of the cross is folly to those who are perishing, but to us who are being saved it is the power of God."

In the second part, verses 19-20, scriptural proof is offered through the second half of the following citation from Isaiah 29:14:

> Therefore, behold, I will again
>   do marvelous things with this people,
>   wonderful and marvelous;
> and the wisdom of their wise men shall perish,
>   and the discernment of their discerning
>   men shall be hid.[2]

Paul is emphasizing here that Scripture already speaks of God's destroying human wisdom. In addition, verse 20 recalls other passages from Isaiah that juxtapose the way the wise, the learned, and the clever thinkers of this world act and the way God acts (see Isaiah 19:11-12; 31:1-3).

After the confirmation from Scripture, we find the theological motive for Paul's thesis in the third part, verses 21-24: God has offered a counter approach. Since people did not come to know God through their human wisdom, he presented himself on the cross, which is a "stumbling block" and "folly."

The fourth part is his conclusion about wisdom. First of all, he makes a general affirmation: "For the foolishness of God is wiser than men, and the weakness of God is stronger than men" (verse 25). This reversal of values has become, so to speak, the law of the economy of salvation.

Two examples follow.

The first concerns the community in verses 26-31: "Consider your call, brethren. . . ." There are few people among you who are wise, powerful, and nobly born. You are simple, humble, poor people; you are servants, slaves, and workers. And yet God has chosen you. This very description of the community illustrates the reversal of the values that God has established in his plan of salvation.

The second example concerns Paul himself (2:1-5): I, too, am not wise or powerful in the eyes of the world but came among you in "fear and trembling." From the Acts of the Apostles, we know that the apostle was returning from a defeat, his failure in Athens. He arrived in Corinth full of weakness, but God gave his words power.

This is how his argument concludes, but it proceeds in an altogether different vein in verse 6: "Yet among the mature we do impart wisdom . . . a secret and hidden wisdom of God." He lifts up wisdom as mystical understanding of the mysteries of God, given by the Spirit.

Points for the *Meditatio*

For the *meditatio* now, I offer three avenues for reflection summarized in three questions:

■ What is the significance of the text we have read for the history of Paul's preaching and his way of carrying out his ministry?

■ What does it mean for the Church's understanding of itself in our time?

■ What does it mean for our lives and for our testimony?

The Significance for Paul's Journey

In this passage Paul reflects on his preaching style in Corinth, so we can ask him, "After the failure in Athens, what did you discover in Corinth about your style of preaching and the carrying out of your ministry? What became clear to you in Corinth beginning in the winter of A.D. 50?"

Paul did indeed attain a more profound understanding of the doctrine of the cross and of its consequences for preaching and for ministry as he became more mature in faith after a certain set of apostolic experiences. Paul might explain the change in the following way:

At the beginning I, too, preached the way Peter did at Pentecost (see Acts 2) or after the healing of the lame man (see Acts 3). I began with the resurrection and preached the glory of God revealed in the risen Christ, or I preached about a miracle as a sign of Jesus' resurrection. I mentioned the death of Jesus, but that was never the central focus of my presentations. Jesus' death was simply one link in a chain of events, although it was a critical link, but my central focus was the resurrection through which God reveals his faithfulness to his promises, a faithfulness that makes up for the stumbling block of the ignominious cross of Jesus. The resurrection was God's justice for the injustice perpetrated on Christ. However, when I no longer needed to preach to the Jews—who needed to know that the prophecies were fulfilled in Christ crucified and glorified—but was preaching only to pagans after the crisis at Antioch in Pisidia (see Acts 13:46-47), I found myself facing a very difficult question. It is the same question that each of you asks whenever you start to talk to nonbelievers or to the nonbelieving part in every person's heart: where do I begin?

In the early days of the church, for example at Lystra (see Acts 14:15-17), because of the misunderstanding of the pagans who thought I was a god that had descended to earth, I improvised a discourse based on wisdom and eloquence (see 1 Corinthians 1:17). I did not dare speak about the resurrection or the cross but limited myself to outlining God's plan in general. I developed that discourse, especially in Athens, in the hopes of finding an approach typical of philosophical wisdom, appealing to the unknown god and hardly mentioning the resurrection or the name of Jesus (see Acts 17:22-31). The failure of my preaching to the philosophers in Athens disappointed me greatly and forced me to reflect more profoundly on the core of Christian catechesis. A decisive change in my apostolate came about from this, i.e., the turning point at Corinth, full of consequences for you, for your life, and for preaching. What exactly happened at Corinth? As I began to approach the Corinthians, marked by the typical vice and skepticism of a large city, I received an insight about how to carry out my apostolate among the pagans. I understood that the principal and persuasive argument for Christian conversion was the cross. The primary argument is not the one founded on fear of imminent divine judgment—as it was for John the Baptist and as I had presented in Athens: God "commands all men everywhere to repent, because he has fixed a day on which he will judge the world" (Acts 17:30-31). I also realized the primary argument was not the one that begins with the glory of Christ, the glory that is expressed in the resurrection of the dead and in the miracles that make that glory present, even though I have always included that theme. I understood, in brief, that the crucifixion of the Messiah—and the merciful love of the Father that it reveals—is the determining factor for the conversion of the heart.

What is being said here could bring to mind some sections of the gospels: the conversion of Zacchaeus, the conversion of the sinful woman in Simon's house, the conversion of the good thief. These are conversions of people who surrendered themselves to the amazing love of God. The prodigal son did not convert when, gripped by hunger, he decided to return to his father's house with sadness and fear. That decision was only the beginning of his conversion; I would call it a change of direction, the beginning of a return. He is actually converted when the father goes out to meet him and embraces him. This is the gesture that signifies the triumph of the mystery of the cross and reveals the amazing mercy of God.

To conclude, in 1 Corinthians 1:17–2:5 St. Paul reports that his preaching experience in that city brought him a very clear and vivid insight: the initial proclamation to those who are far from God must, first and foremost, make known God's mercy as demonstrated through the mystery of the cross. It must make people aware of the intimate paternal and maternal love of God that comes to meet us despite our resistance.

This is the kind of preaching that fully brings to light God's mercy in the expiating death of his Son on Calvary and God's omnipotence that manifests itself in forgiving and saving that which was lost.

Again, Paul is saying to us,

> In Corinth, people's conversion, their attention, their surprise, their joy—when they understood my proclamation—confirmed to me that the cross, far from being weakness, the weakness of God, is actually a re-creating power for believers and the formative principle of solid and mature personalities. Far from being foolishness, it is the wisdom of God, the principle of a new understanding of things that is capable of constituting a new order and a new humanity. I also experienced how the most culturally dispossessed people and the most deprived people understood the language of the cross and were converted.

As the answer to our first question, we can summarize that while he was evangelizing the Corinthians, Paul understood and experienced the spiritual power of the crucifixion of the Son of God to bring about profound conversions among pagans called to the faith.

The Face of the Church Today

What does all this mean for the Church's understanding of itself today? What does this Pauline text mean for the life of our Church today?

Allow me to quote the theologian Ghislain Lafont, recalling a talk he gave at a diocesan pastoral council regarding the face of the church today.

First of all, he listed its most vital and lively aspects: concern for the poor, expressed not only through charity but through many other forms that aim to help the poor take charge of their lives, organize themselves, become fully responsible as individuals and as communities; diocesan synods with the participation of the laity; the commitment of believers to transmit the faith; the emergence of new communities that want to live the gospel in a radical way; openness to dialogue; the richness of contemporary theology (he commented that it is difficult to find in the church's history a century as rich with great theologians as the twentieth century); the presence of prophets (he mentions Martin Luther King, Monsignor Romero, Cardinal Hume, and others); and the presence of martyrs, perhaps more numerous than in times past (the Trappist monks killed in Algeria and so many other missionaries that we know who have died for their faith).

After this list, he adds,

It seems to me that there is a very definite significance to this number of activities and, at the same time, to the humility in the features of the face of the church. At any point in history, the face of the church cannot be different than the face of the Christ who prevails in the consciousness of Christians. The image of Jesus that prevails at the present time seems to be that of the servant, the Lamb of God, the man of the beatitudes, along with the radical insight that his humility is not just linked to the requirements for redemption from sins but, more significantly, that it belongs to the very essence of Christ. . . . Christian devotion and theology in our day arises from contemplation of the Lamb who was slain and goes on from there to contemplation of the blessed Trinity. If God is love, we cannot speak only about his glory and omnipotence, but we also need to speak about his gift, about his acceptance of us, and—with all the qualifications needed in using these words—about his humility and poverty.[3]

This kind of analysis is an application of St. Paul's passage. It is not an attempt to rationalize the failures of the Church. Starting with Christ, the sacrificed Lamb, it sees in the Church the richness of a presence that is capable of convincing people to look beyond the image of power, strength, and self-sufficiency that the Church projected during certain times in its history.

Our Life and Our Testimony

The last avenue for reflection concerns each of us. What does Paul's text mean for our life and our testimony? The answer can only be a personal one. It means knowing how to come before the mystery of the cross in prayer and to ascertain in its light how much of the weakness of God is given to us to experience. It means knowing how to look at the discomforts and the inconveniences of life through the eyes of faith. It means knowing how to look at the problems in the church with an awareness of the fruitfulness of the cross.

Even though it may seem quick, this is a path that we walk very slowly. In terms of the heart, even Paul required considerable time to reach the fullness of this insight expressed in the First Letter to the Corinthians.

1. Cardinal Carlo M. Martini, *Parlo al tuo cuore: Per una regola di vita del cristiano ambrosiano* [I Speak to Your Heart: The Rule for Christian Life According to Ambrose], pastoral letter for 1996–1997, September 8, 1996.

2. In both the Italian and the English translations of the Bible, the wording of the quote from Isaiah in 1 Corinthians 1:19 is different from the wording of the passage where it occurs in the Old Testament.

3. Ghislain Lafont, *La diaconia è il vero futuro della chiesa* [The Diaconate Is the Real Future of the Church], March 2000, no. 114.

CHAPTER 9

The Ministry of Reconciliation

I will be dealing with a *lectio* of the central portion of Paul's Second Letter to the Corinthians. A famous Scripture scholar, Fr. Ferdinand Prat, said this about the letter:

> Paul has written nothing more eloquent, more heartfelt, or more passionate than this Epistle. Sadness and joy, fear and hope, tenderness and indignation vibrate through its pages with equal intensity. The art of exalting the most ordinary incidents by applying to them the loftiest principles of faith makes of it an inexhaustible mine for lovers of asceticism and mysticism.[1]

Before reflecting on the section in which the apostle speaks about the ministry of the new covenant, we should pay attention to the whole context, reading the end of chapter 3 and all of chapters 4 and 5.

A Reading from 2 Corinthians 5:18-20

Chapter 5 ends with the section for our reflection:

> [18]All this is from God, who through Christ reconciled us to himself and gave us the ministry of reconciliation; [19]that is, God was in Christ was reconciling the world to himself, not counting their trespasses against them, and entrusting to us the message of reconciliation. [20]So we are ambassadors for

Christ, God making his appeal through us. We beseech you on behalf of Christ, be reconciled to God.

Paul identifies the ministry of the new covenant as a ministry of *reconciliation*. This obviously does not point only to the ministry of the Sacrament of Reconciliation but to the ministry of the apostle's whole life, as well.

Structure and Content

The passage contains a general assertion followed by an explanation and the consequences that arise from it.

The assertion consists of a very general principle and two applications. The principle is that "all this is from God." This is christocentrism applied to our understanding of the whole of reality. Everything is from God, through Christ.

The idea that everything comes from God is specified in two ways: *first*, God, "through Christ, reconciled us to himself" (verse 18); and *second*, God entrusted the message of reconciliation to us. The entirety of the divine action is thus summarized in two ways: one pertains to Christ, and the other pertains to the Church.

This assertion is further clarified when Paul answers these questions: How did God reconcile us through Christ? How does he entrust us with the message of reconciliation?

He has reconciled us in Christ *by forgiving us*: "God was in Christ reconciling the world to himself, not counting their trespasses against them" (verse 19). It is a reconciliation of forgiveness, of mercy. Through the death of Christ, through his death out of love, God has unconditionally accepted the sinner.

This is how Paul describes the act of the covenant, adding new emphasis with respect to the way it was described in chapter 3 of the letter. This act of reconciliation is not based on the fact that a person has done penance, has become converted, or has restored to God the honor that he or she had taken away from him. It is a unilateral and gratuitous action.

Second, this act of christological reconciliation is expressed in relation to the Church: "entrusting to us the message of reconciliation." It is an act that is mediated through the word of the Church, through the ministry. That aspect gets reemphasized: "We are ambassadors for Christ" (verse 20). We are representatives of Christ the reconciler, representing him who reconciled humanity through his flesh. "God [is] making his appeal through us" (verse 20). We are agents of a specific mandate entrusted to us. And his mandate is summarized in a statement that expresses the message of reconciliation in a straightforward way: "We beseech you on behalf of Christ, be reconciled to God" (verse 20). Some translations say, "Let yourselves be reconciled to God," as if to say, God has already done his part to be reconciled with you, and all you need to do is to let God have his way; let him finish out his work of reconciliation.

This is the structure of the passage. Earlier in chapter 3 the ministry of the new covenant was presented in a positive and creative way as the ministry of the Spirit, bringing life, enthusiasm, and spiritual progress. It is now presented in a new light as the ministry of reparation, restitution, reconciliation.

Meditatio

Let us try to understand what Paul means, what the fundamental points of his message are, and what significance they have for us today.

I will proceed by listing several brief theses that express in doctrinal form the content of this rich and moving text in which Paul emphasizes his conviction about being a minister of reconciliation.

First thesis. The new covenant is a covenant of reconciliation. God wants to establish a very intimate, spousal, enduring, and eternal relationship with the human race, through which he and the human race become one, as Christ's humanity is one with the word. However, this covenant is also a reestablishment of a broken relationship. This is what characterizes the new covenant and what helps us understand why its center is the mystery of the cross. It is not simply an action of God meant to improve our situation, but rather a restorative act to set right a broken world, to reestablish a bond that had been torn and broken, to restore a relationship that had been undermined and weakened.

The ministry of reconciliation is difficult precisely because it is a ministry that involves restoration. We are not dealing here with the spousal image of a marriage between two pure and innocent young people, approved by their respective parents, which moves ahead well and brings their union to completion. We are dealing instead with a broken marriage that needs to have a new rapport established. That is why the new covenant is hard work.

Second thesis. This new covenant presupposes the sinfulness of the human race and moral decadence in history. Let us recall Jesus' pessimistic words about life in this world when he says, "You then, who are evil, know how to give good gifts to your children" (Luke 11:13); his premise here is that people are evil. "O faithless and perverse generation, how long am I to be with you? How long am I to bear with you?" (Matthew 17:17): Jesus starts with the premise of a generation whose relationship with God is broken and weak, which is the case for individuals and for all of humanity. According to John Paul II's encyclical *Sollicitudo rei socialis*,[2] the structures of sin have undermined the fabric of human relationships, leaving human beings prey to ambitions, hate, egotism, pride, and religious and moral darkness. This is the starting point for the new covenant, and because of that, we find ourselves before a heroic enterprise: *Exultavit ut gigas ad currendam viam* ("Like a strong man [he] runs [his] course with joy" [Psalm 19:5]). This is a restorative enterprise for a situation that until now was irreparably damaged.

Third thesis. Consequently, this new covenant of reconciliation is a new creative act: "Therefore, if any one is in Christ, he is a new creation; the old has passed away, behold, the new has come" (2 Corinthians 5:17).

Creation was good, but because it has been damaged, everything needs to be remade. The new covenant is a remaking of humanity; it involves a restoration of the broken human spirit to its original condition. This is why it is an extraordinary act and not a simple improvement for the human race. It is a true re-creation of the human spirit.

Fourth thesis. As a result, we understand that *this action on God's part occurs through the death of Christ out of love.* This rebirth of humanity is so staggering that it requires the death and resurrection of Jesus. And, as Paul says, "The love of Christ controls us, because we are convinced that one has died for all; therefore all have died. And he died for all, that those who live might live no longer for themselves but for him who for their sake died and was raised" (2 Corinthians 5:14-15).

The new covenant is a new creation, a new beginning starting with the resurrection of the crucified One and with our incorporation into the death and resurrection of Jesus. Therefore, the crucified One is its central figure, demonstrating the love of God that gives itself to the very end and that forgives to the very end. Coming from a position of unconditional forgiveness and love, he re-creates the new humanity through his resurrection.

Fifth thesis. Our ministry, the ministry of reconciliation, involves the reconstruction of fragile and broken personalities. Therefore, it is a very difficult and weighty task with ongoing temptations to weariness and discouragement.

Even after baptism, personalities remain weakened, although people have the possibility, the grace, of living a new life. We labor under the weight of human weakness and the influence of the flesh. Even though the personality is re-created *in principle* through the cross of Christ and in baptism, its *de facto* re-creation constitutes a slow process.

Such a process is not only slow but also all-encompassing, because it means being reconciled with oneself, one's destiny, one's life, one's health, one's defects, one's surroundings, one's family, and society.

The covenant of reconciliation enables us to recover our delight in being children of the Father, being brothers and sisters together, being people who are forgiven and loved and who joyfully think of themselves as forgiven and loved.

This is the ministry of reconciliation: a ministry of the patient reconstruction of personalities who go from being weak and inconsistent to being at peace, capable now of a righteous relationship with God, with absolute mystery, with one's own poverty, with whatever pettiness exists in one's environment, and with the world, however grim and disorderly it may be.

The covenant of reconciliation creates personalities who lovingly accept themselves and others because God has established an eternal spousal relationship that defines us, that describes us, that gives us strength and allows us to express ourselves peacefully and integrate ourselves with our surroundings. This covenant has been made between human beings and God; between brothers and sisters; between man and woman; between human beings and the earth.

Our ministry is the ministry of this new covenant, the service of restoring the personalities of individuals and groups by the power of God. Without God's pardon, without his mercy, and without the gift of the Spirit who renews us, all of this would merely be wishful thinking. It is the grace of the Spirit that renews people's hearts and makes them capable of accepting themselves, of accepting others, of feeling themselves loved, and of expressing themselves with solidarity and fraternity. It is the grace of the Spirit that inaugurates the new covenant.

Sixth thesis. Our ministry is essentially one of encouragement, according to what Paul says: "We beseech you on behalf of Christ, be reconciled to God" (verse 20). I do not mean encouragement in the sense of saying that everything is fine, but that even if things are not fine, there is a hope for you, there is a life of peace and harmony for you, there is a fullness of human and divine satisfaction for you. Let yourselves be reconciled to God, to the people around you, to your work, to your sicknesses, to your troubles, to your mental and emotional exhaustion—to everything you dislike in yourselves. Let yourselves be reconciled through reconciliation to God.

Seventh thesis. Our ministry is rooted in understanding, compassion, and mercy. It is a ministry of peace—Fr. Bernard Häring has a good book on confession called *Shalom*[3]—because it is a ministry that tries to understand the depths of the human heart, its sufferings, its ignorance, its resistance, and tries to approach it with sympathy, empathy, and mercy, to help people on their way, to help them take small steps. These are not steps that simply absolve or justify everything; but rather, they encourage people to keep going, because in spite of other things, their lives are now opened, and they are able to take one more step.

Eighth thesis. This kind of ministry also includes sternness and severity. It does not consist only of gentle kindness. In fact, we see that Jesus, the model for this ministry who can act with unheard-of compassion, knows how to assume a stern and severe tone when necessary. Paul also links compassion and severity:

> I speak as to children—widen your hearts also [a compassionate tone here]. Do not be mismated with unbelievers. For what partnership have righteousness and iniquity? Or what fellowship has light with darkness? What accord has Christ with Belial? Or what has a believer in common with an unbeliever? What agreement has the temple of God with idols? (2 Corinthians 6:13-16a)

Paul is speaking forcefully here, precisely because of his compassion: the covenant is based on the jealous love of a God who does not accept rivals. The law of the covenant is therefore the law of the exclusive, jealous love of the one and only God. In this light, we can understand some of Jesus' statements: "Woe to whoever causes one of these little ones to sin; it would be better for him to have a millstone around his neck and be drowned in the depths of the sea" (see Matthew 18:6; Mark 9:42; Luke 17:2) and "I never knew you; depart from me, you evildoers" (Matthew 7:23).

When our ministry is truly rooted in us, we also encounter times like these, precisely because of the ministry of covenant. "Since we have these promises, beloved, let us cleanse ourselves from every defilement of body and spirit, and make holiness perfect in the fear of God" (2 Corinthians 7:1). It is a ministry of holiness. Not a legal holiness, imposed from on high with rigidity, anger, or reproach, but a holiness that comes about through love and compassion.

Particular Occasions of Reconciliation

The ministry of reconciliation is active throughout our lives but especially on two different occasions.

The *first occasion* is that of intercession during the Eucharist. We priests perform this ministry when we offer the body and blood of Christ and present him to the people. It is the supreme moment in which we are ministers of reconciliation: "Behold the Lamb of God who takes away the sins of the world." If only people understood the extraordinary quality of this action and these words! We often complain about the sins of the world, the stories in the newspapers full of crime, atrocity, and vulgarity, but still we say, "Behold him who takes away the sins of the world!" We thus affirm the certainty of the re-creation of this world immersed in sin. During the offering and eucharistic intercession, when we pray with the church for the Lord to deliver his people from every evil, discord, and hostility, we are ministers of reconciliation.

The *second occasion* is that of sacramental reconciliation in which God restores a person through a free and creative act. Even though this ministry is subject to negative conditions that can be a source of suffering, such as hastiness, it is nonetheless enormously valuable, because it is miraculous that a human being can obtain forgiveness from God for very grave offenses that are capable of destroying a human psyche.

Reconciliation with Ourselves

Finally, the *ministry of reconciliation has to do especially with ourselves,* because we cannot give peace if we do not have it. We cannot minister reconciliation if we are not ourselves reconciled. To be reconciled does not mean that we have nothing to forgive anybody; it means that we *do* have things to forgive and that we *do* forgive—ourselves and others. It is actually easy to feel reconciled when no one owes us a debt. If, instead, we have credits or debts—whether with ourselves, with others, or with the Church—then we need that experience of being reconciled within ourselves. This often takes a long time, because daily circumstances, without our realizing it, lead us to continual states of slight animosity, bad moods, negative judgments, or irritations that we perhaps hardly pay attention to and that, little by little, become large knots. One way to loosen these knots of bitterness, malaise, or discontent is the exercise of *lectio divina* that should never be absent from our daily routine.

We are thus the primary subjects of the ministry of reconciliation, and we should turn to Mary often for her help, for she is the mother of reconciliation.

To conclude, I would like to recall Jesus' words on the cross when, at the end of his ministry, he entrusted Mary to John and

John to Mary. This action serves as a sign of the reconciliation that has been accomplished and uses a covenant formula: "You are my people, and I am your God" becomes "You are my mother, and I am your son; this is now your son, and this is now your mother."

The covenant is summarized in the mysterious relationship between the disciple and Mary. In the mutual entrusting of the disciple *to* Mary, there is a sort of foretaste, an ongoing guarantee that the mystery of the covenant resolves all the divisions and the contradictions within us.

I encourage you then to reflect on the power of this mystery, a simple symbol of the covenant of reconciliation and of the spousal intimacy that enters into our hearts and forms them with peace, compassion, serenity, and interior joy.

1. Ferdinand Prat, *The Theology of Saint Paul*, trans. John L. Stoddard, 11th ed., vol. 1 (Westminster, MD: Chicago: Newman Bookshop, 1952), 142.

2. Pope John Paul II, *Sollicitudo rei socialis* [On Social Concern], Dec. 30, 1987.

3. Bernhard Häring, *Shalom: Peace: The Sacrament of Reconciliation*, rev. ed. (Garden City, NY: Image Books, 1969).

Sources

The chapters in this book are excerpts adapted from the following books published by Ancora Editrice:

1. Paul's Conversion
"La conoscenza di Gesù," in Carlo M. Martini, *Le confessione di Paolo: Meditazioni,* 2003, 29–42.

2. The Passion of Paul
"Passio Pauli, passio Christi," in Carlo M. Martini, *Le confessione di Paolo: Meditazioni,* 2003, 123–138.

3. Paul's Transfiguration
"La trasfigurazione di Paolo," in Carlo M. Martini, *Le confessione di Paolo: Meditazioni,* 2003, 107–121.

4. The Mystery of the Church
"Come Cristo ha amato la Chiesa e ha dato se stesso per lei (Ef. 5:25): L'amore per la Chiesa nel ministero di Gesù e nel nostro," in Carlo M. Martini, Elena Ascoli, Luigi Bettazzi, *Si può amare la Chiesa? Dedizione e parresia nel ministero,* 2000, 75–90.

5. Love for the Community
"Voi siete una lettera di Cristo composta da noi" (2 Cor. 3:3): La passione di servire lo Spirito nei cuori," in Carlo M. Martini, Godfried Danneels, Benoît Standaert, *Lo spirito dell'apostolo: Quando il ministero ha un'anima,* 2002, 83–96.

6. Suffering and Consolation
"Sofferenze e consolazioni," in Carlo M. Martini, *Paolo nel vivo del ministero*, 1990, 9–25.

7. The Mystery of Iniquity
"Nel 'mistero dell'iniquità' (2 Ts. 2:7)," in Carlo M. Martini, Carla Bettinelli, Guido Formigoni, *L'assurdo di Auschwitz e il mistero della croce*, 2001, 19–36.

8. The Word of the Cross
"Potenza e sapienza dell'uomo, debolezza e stoltezza di Dio: Obbedienza e resistenza alla 'parola della croce,'" in Raniero Cantalamessa and Carlo M. Martini, *Dalla Croce la perfetta letizia: Francesco d'Assisi parla ai preti*, 2001, 81–98.

9. The Ministry of Reconciliation
"Il ministero della nuova alleanza come ministero della reconciliazione," in Carlo M. Martini, *Paolo nel vivo del ministero*, 1990, 59–70.